Understanding Spirit,
Understanding Yourself

P.O. Box 2752
Kennebunkport, ME 04046
ISBN: 1-59109-884-x
Understanding Spirit, Understanding Yourself: Two Journeys Of Self-Discovery
Through Spirit Communication / by Bob Olson & Vicki Monroe
Cover Photo: Govert Jan Mennen
Trade paperback
1. New Age / Metaphysical, 2. Death / Grief / Loss, 3. Spiritualism

BOB OLSON &
VICKI MONROE

UNDERSTANDING SPIRIT, UNDERSTANDING YOURSELF

Two Journeys
Of Self-Discovery Through
Spirit Communication

2003

Understanding Spirit, Understanding Yourself

ABOUT THE AUTHORS

VICKI MONROE, spirit messenger, spreads her healing message that life is eternal through her public demonstrations on stage, radio and television, through her private readings, and now through her new book, Understanding Spirit, Understanding Yourself: Two Journeys Of Self-Discovery Through Spirit Communication.

Vicki receives messages in several ways from spirits and spirit guides: by seeing them, hearing them, hearing them telepathically, seeing mental-symbolic images in her mind, feeling physical sensations in her body, and experiencing emotional feelings sent by spirits. Vicki Monroe is also a doctor of natural medicine, which is helpful when communicating spirit messages involving matters of health and healing.

Vicki has been interviewed or featured by numerous television, radio and print media including:

PRINT: Down East magazine / Portland City Life magazine / The Boston Globe / Maine Sunday Telegram / The Phoenix Sun (voted "Best Psychic Advisor") / Spirit Of Change magazine / Portsmouth Herald.

TELEVISION: The Jenny Jones Show / Bill Greene's Maine on NBC / WGAN Morning Show on ABC / NBC Portland Maine with Kevin Kelley / UPN's Our Maine / Channel 6 Maine News / Channel 13 Maine news.

RADIO: Boston's WBZ, The Jordan Rich Show / Palm Spring's KPSI, Joey English / Boston's WBCN, Mat Schaffer / Worcester's WTAG News Radio / The Spirit Communication Hour, Cable Radio Network & Talk America / Portland, Maine's WJBQ Morning Show, every Thursday for three years.

Vicki may be contacted via her website, VickiMonroe.com (www.vickimonroe.com), or by calling her office at 207-499-0067.

BOB OLSON, former skeptic, is an author, lecturer, magazine writer and editor. He writes and lectures on the subjects of grief healing, spirit communication, life after death, and the spiritual principles of living a joyful, successful and fulfilling life.

Bob is the author of *Understanding Spirit, Understanding Yourself: Two Journeys Of Self-Discovery Through Spirit Communication* and *Win The Battle: The 3 Step Lifesaving Formula To Conquer Depression And Bipolar Disorder.* He is currently writing his next book about grief healing.

Bob is also the editor of OfSpirit.com Magazine (www.ofspirit.com) and founder of BestPsychicMediums.com (www.bestpsychicmediums.com) and GriefAndBelief.com (www.griefandbelief.com). These Internet resources provide thousands of pages of articles, interviews, links and practitioner profiles to millions of visitors each year.

Bob has been interviewed or featured by numerous television, radio and print media including:

PRINT: US News & World Report / Family Circle / Redbook / Women's Day / Down East magazine / Worcester Telegram / Spirit Of Change magazine / The Boston Globe / Metrowest Daily News / Portsmouth Herald.

TELEVISION: New England Cable News, Boston / Newswatch Three TV, Worcester / WSBK TV, City Stories, Boston / WCVB TV 5, HealthBeat, Boston / Greater Media TV with James Ellis, Massachusetts.

RADIO: Talk America, Dana Sylvia / KPSI AM, Just Joey / WEW AM, Licia Terranova / WKRC AM Jeri, Tom & Craig / KXRK FM, Bob Salter / WBZ AM, The Jordan Rich Show / WBZ AM, Deb Lawlor / WIP AM, Peter Solomon / WDRC AM, Brad Davis / KERI AM, Martin Garza / KCMN AM, Tron Simpson / KXTQ FM, Vikki Robbins / KCBS AM, Barb Blum / WBOS FM, David O'Leary / WSJZ FM, Hillary Stevens / WBAA AM, Dan Skinner / WXLO FM, Joni Sciani / WRKO AM, That Guy Tai / KPLX FM, Chris Sommer / WROR FM, Judy Papparelli / WBCN FM, Mat Schaefer / KOA AM, Rick Barber / KEZK FM, Kris Kelly / KINN AM, Mike Shinaberry / WRSC AM, Jeff Byers / WODS FM, June Knight / WTAG AM, George Brown / WTAG AM, The John Alexandrov Show / WVNE AM, Eleanor Hubbard / The Spirit Communication Hour Cable Radio Network & Talk America.

Bob may be contacted via his website, OfSpirit.com (www.ofspirit.com), or by calling his office at 207-967-9892.

CONTENTS

ACKNOWLEDGMENTS

We are grateful to everyone who has helped us to learn, grow and spread our message of hope, including our family, friends, colleagues, loved ones in spirit and spirit guides. We are especially appreciative of the patience and support we received from Bret and Melissa.

To Our Fathers Who Watch Over Us From Above

INTRODUCTION
OVERLAPPING JOURNEYS

"You can preach a better sermon with your life than with your lips."

~ Oliver Goldsmith

There is a famous quote by Oliver Goldsmith that reads, "You can preach a better sermon with your life than with your lips." That quote is the premise upon which this book was written. Based on the paths of two very different people—a skeptic and a spirit messenger—this book teaches about the power of spirit to transform your life.

While reading this book, you will be taken on a journey as Bob Olson, the skeptic, and Vicki Monroe, the spirit messenger, share with you the private details of their own individual, yet overlapping, journeys toward understanding spirit. When you have completed this book you will not only be more educated about spirits, the spirit world and spirit communication, but you will also be more aware of the power of your *human* spirit. Successful living is not solely about remembering your spiritual self (Bob's journey), nor is it solely about discovering your human self (Vicki's journey); but rather, it is about finding a balance between the two.

The chapters that follow are like two books in one. Bob Olson's chapters will teach you about the experiences, revelations and lessons that transformed him from cynical skeptic to spiritual knower by incorporating stories about his investigation into the world of spirit communication. Vicki Monroe's chapters are more biographical, sharing with you her extraordinary experiences as a spirit messenger (psychic medium) growing up and "coming out" in a skeptical world. Vicki's story will inspire anyone dealing with issues of adversity, discrimination, fear or personal empowerment.

Within these stories about Bob and Vicki are three themes: One, the theme of friendship between two people who were undoubtedly destined to teach one another various lessons in this lifetime; Two, the theme of understanding spirit, which Vicki learned early in life and Bob needed to acquire; and Three, the theme of understanding human spirit, which Bob learned early in life and Vicki needed to acquire.

The underlying message of this book is that life is about balance, balancing matters of Spirit with matters of human spirit. We can't live in this world focused on just one or the other. We are originally from Spirit, yet we are living inside human bodies among a society of human beings. Even the adage that says, "We are not human beings having a spiritual experience, but rather spiritual beings having a human experience," does not mean we must only focus on the spiritual. It means we must remember the importance of both.

PART I
The Initiation

CHAPTER ONE
A VISIT FROM HEAVEN

By Vicki Monroe

How like an angel came I down!
How bright are all things here!
When first among his works I did appear,
Oh, how their glory did me crown!
The world resembled his eternity,
In which my soul did walk;
And ev'rything that I did see
Did with me talk.
~ Thomas Traherne

My name is Vicki Monroe and I call myself a "spirit messenger." There was a time when I didn't know what to call myself in relation to my ability to communicate with spirits. Some people were using the term "psychic medium," which is accurate, but most people didn't know what that meant at the time. My friend, Bob Olson, whom you will hear from in the next chapter, thought the term "spirit messenger" more accurately described what I do—I communicate messages from people "in spirit" to people like you. Well, that was back in 1999 and the phrase just kind of stuck.

CHILDHOOD GIFT OR FREAKISH DISABILITY?

I wasn't always a spirit messenger. For most of my childhood, I was content with just seeing and hearing spirits. I certainly wasn't relaying messages from spirits to anyone here on the earth plane. Well, I did tell some people about the spirits I saw, but that didn't go too well. So at some point in my childhood, I learned to ignore my ability because of all the flack I was getting about it. Instead of feeling like my ability to see spirits was a gift, most people made me feel like it was some freakish disability.

Looking back, I don't know if *anyone* really believed me when I told them what I saw. I know some people were afraid of what I told them, thinking that if my ability was real that it might just be evil. The kids I told about it basically just teased me. "Oh, here comes the ghost lady," they would say, causing the other kids to start laughing at me. The adults in my life didn't tease me so much as appease me. They thought I had an overactive imagination. So I didn't grow up feeling special because of my ability; I felt odd and outcast. Resultantly, by the time I became a teenager, I stopped talking about the spirits I saw. In fact, I began trying to ignore these pestering visions altogether.

My ability to see spirits never stopped, but if you ignore any gift long enough—like music, art or writing—it will eventually stop being a part of your daily life. It's sort of like when people live by the ocean or the mountains, after a while they stop noticing the majestic beauty of it all. They get caught up in the busyness of life, driving to and from work every day and rarely noticing what photographers and painters spend their lives trying to capture.

Consequently, by the time I was twenty-three, I was barely aware of my spirit sightings anymore. Besides, I was raising two young boys in a foreign country—Germany—while my husband, Bret, an Air Force Sergeant, worked for missile maintenance systems (whatever that means) for twelve hours a day. Heck, I was too busy living in *this* world to be focusing on people from another one. At least that's what I thought.

FAMILY VISITS FROM MAINE

After a year in Germany, I was missing my family back home in Maine. The Air Force had already shipped us around the United States for four years before being shipped out to Germany. I come from a pretty close family, so I didn't like being away so long. But Bret and I got news from my brother, Chuck, that he and his wife, Linda, were coming to Germany to celebrate their first anniversary. It was a last minute decision, made just three days before they arrived. I couldn't have been more excited.

On the second morning after their arrival, we were all just hanging around the house. I was cleaning up after breakfast, Linda was drying her hair in the bathroom and the two boys and two men were watching cartoons on television. I left the kitchen and walked into the bedroom, immediately smelling a strong scent of perfume. I called Linda to ask what fragrance she was wearing. She said she hadn't brought any perfume to Germany, as she walked into the bedroom to smell it.

"That's Halston?" said Linda, "You know who wears that?"

"Who?" I said.

"Heather. She wears it all the time," she said.

Linda and my younger sister, Heather, were close friends so Linda was sure it was the same perfume she smelled. Then, just as she finished saying it, the phone rang. Linda walked back into the bathroom as I answered the phone. It was my father calling from Maine.

"It's Dad," I told Bret and Chuck, who were staring at me to see who had called.

"Oh, it's the Chief! He's calling to find out how everything's going," said Chuck.

Then Bret looked at me and his faced dropped. "It's three o'clock in the morning there," he said.

"I have some bad news," said my father.

I hesitated, "What?"

"We lost Heather and Tom tonight," he answered (Tom is Heather's husband).

I didn't grasp it. "What do you mean lost?" I said.

"They died in a car accident, honey."

I repeated my father's words to everyone before feeling the impact behind the words. "Heather and Tom got killed tonight in a car accident." Then I sat there with the phone to my ear in silence, kind of numb. My father, obviously still in shock himself, said, "I'm sorry, honey. Look, I can't talk now. I'll call you back when I have more information."

"It's okay, Dad. It's going to be okay," I said. And when I hung up, a part of me actually thought it would be. This was the first time I had experienced someone so close to me dying. It didn't seem possible. My parents, Heather and the accident were all so distant from Germany. The reality of it all was very hard for me to grasp. Up until this moment, things in my life always turned out okay. This would be different. My life was about to change in more ways than one, and it would never be the same.

FAMILY VISITS FROM HEAVEN

I wasn't able to cry for two days. I guess I was too disconnected from it, being thousands of miles away and all. On the second night, I finally talked to my mother on the phone. She had learned that Heather and Tom were only a quarter-mile from where they were staying when their tiny car was broadsided by another. The teen driving the other car, with his three teenage buddies, thought it was cool to shut his lights off while speeding through the stop sign. Heather and Tom never saw them coming. The teens survived the accident with minor injuries.

The sound of my mother's voice pierced the dam and got me crying, turning my tearful drought into a tempest. "Will life ever be the same?" I wept.

"With time it will be," she said. I believed Mom's words. I guess I *needed* to believe her. Every thought of a future without my little sister stabbed at my gut. I suddenly had a million questions and absolutely no answers. Why Heather? Why so young? Did she and Tom suffer? Where are they now?

Once the tears started, I couldn't get them to stop. Bret consoled me in bed until I fell asleep in his arms. The next thing I knew I awoke hearing myself saying, "What?" It was like someone yelled my name in a dream and I woke myself answering them. I looked at the clock; it was 2:45 in the morning.

I knew I was supposed to get out of bed and go into the living room. I don't know how I knew this; I just knew. At first I tried being quiet so I wouldn't wake up Bret; but again, I somehow knew that he wasn't going to wake up regardless of how much noise I made. As I walked into the living room, Chuck and Linda were to my right sleeping on the pullout sofa bed. Again, I somehow knew they would not wake up. I looked at the cuckoo clock and noticed it had stopped ticking at 2:45.

I also knew I wasn't dreaming, although everything was strangely surreal. I felt a presence to my left and as I turned my head I saw my sister, Heather, sitting in Bret's recliner. Her husband, Tom, was sitting on the floor in front of her with his legs crossed. I'll never forget what she was wearing: a fuchsia blouse, denim blue jeans and matching fuchsia heels. Tom had a big cream-colored wool sweater on with jeans and sneakers. They were obviously sitting there waiting for me.

My first thought was "What a relief. It's not true. You didn't die after all." Then Heather stood up and I saw this iridescent glow around her. They both had this radiating beauty about them that was far beyond what was normal. I stood there in the living room sort of stunned, taking in this vision. Then it occurred to me that they had really passed. They were obviously no longer of this world.

Heather didn't say anything, but walked toward me and put her arms around me. I could actually feel her as we embraced, but it was more than just physical; it was like I could feel her essence through every cell in my body, a soothing energy of warmth, love and peace. As she hugged me, every joyous memory of our entire life together instantly flashed through my mind. I could feel her overwhelming love for me and all the wonderful feelings we shared together bursting through into one single moment. It was a moment I hoped would never stop. My face was smothered in joyful tears.

Tom got up slowly as Heather released her heavenly hold on me. She stood back as he then greeted me with a hug. Again, I felt a burst of loving energy, although not with the same intensity I received from Heather. Then I heard his voice in my head, yet his mouth didn't move. He was communicating with me by thought.

"Now that you know we are here, why don't you have a seat? We have some things to talk about," he said. Tom was point blank, gentle but serious like we needed to get down to business. I looked at Heather. She nodded at me as they each sat down. I sat on a sofa that wasn't being used by Chuck and Linda, who continued to sleep soundly on the other side of the room. I wiped the tears off my face as I snuggled among some pillows, still sniffling.

A million questions went through my mind, "What happened? Was it your time to go? Did you suffer? Heather and Tom heard my thoughts.

"Slow down," said Heather, "Yes, it was our time to go. When the accident happened, I immediately left my body. No suffering. That is what normally happens. The spirit will leave the body before impact when death is imminent."

Then I asked, "Did you go into the light? Were relatives waiting for you? Did you have your life review? What is it like there?"

Tom looked at me affectionately and said, "Yes, all those things. But, Vicki, you don't have to ask. You already know the answers. Do you remember those conversations we used to have about life-after-death? And all that atheist crap I used to talk about?" I nodded affirmatively. I remembered the long conversations Tom and I used to have about life after death and spirituality. "Well, you were so right," he said, "I'm sorry I didn't believe you. Your experiences have taught you more than you realize. I need you to know that. And Vicki, it is amazing here."

I don't know if it was the look he gave me, what he told me or something he sent to me energetically, but it felt like my heart wept in bliss—not because I was right and he had been wrong about life-after-death, but because everything I had believed was now being confirmed to me by two people I loved and trusted who had come to me from the afterlife to teach me the truth.

Heather and Tom then told me they had come to teach me about life-after-death and related spiritual matters. This was my moment to ask them any questions I had. They would give me all the answers I needed. They wanted to help me affirm what I already knew and to bring the spiritual insights I had gained from my experiences seeing spirits to a new level of knowing.

I sat on the sofa in silence soaking it all in when Heather interrupted, "Aren't you going to write this stuff down? Her eyes motioned to a pad and pen that was at my side. I don't know if the pad and pen were already there or if Heather and Tom somehow made them appear; but they were real. I picked them up and started writing frantically as I asked them questions with my mind.

"What's it like there?" I asked.

"Don't you remember?" asked Heather.

"No, of course not," I answered.

"That's part of the problem," said Heather, "We forget. We remember at the beginning of life, as children, but we forget as we get older. Yet it isn't necessary to forget. We forget because we never stop to remember. Of course this is perpetuated by a culture that does not teach us to remember. It's like when we wake from a dream. If we jump out of bed and keep moving, we forget what we have dreamed. But if we take a moment upon awakening to remember and contemplate our dreams before jumping out of bed, we remember them forever. This is so unfortunate because not remembering the peace and joyfulness of our true home causes us to feel disconnected and fearful during our life's journey. But we are not alone, Vicki. We are all so much more connected than we know. And you are going to help people to remember this in your upcoming community service (I had no idea what she meant by "community service," but I trusted that I would find out)."

As I got used to communicating with my thoughts, I realized that this was a much faster means of communication. Questions and answers signaled back and forth in rapid fire. What might normally take minutes to say verbally, took only seconds by thought. Moreover, this was a different kind of learning than anything I had ever experienced. It was not like learning from a book or classroom, where we memorize information with repetitive recitation. Everything Heather and Tom taught me was absorbed instantly and I immediately knew it to be truth. Although I wrote some stuff down, I noticed that taking notes was actually slowing me down, so I wrote sparingly.

Three hours passed in what seemed like twenty minutes. I had pages of notes, but wondered why I needed them since all the information was firmly in my head. There were no goodbyes with Heather and Tom. I knew I would see them again, although I did not know when. Suddenly, around 5:45 AM, I found myself in my bedroom doorway. My first thought was that it was all just a dream. Then I saw the pad and pen and all my notes. I was so happy that I woke Bret up and told him all about my visit that evening. He seemed to believe me, but he may have been accommodating me due to my earlier state of despair.

I have seen Heather and Tom about fifteen or twenty more times since this first visit. Sometimes it was Heather alone. It's hard to know the exact number because many were short visits. Yet every one had a purpose. Some visits were for single lessons; some conveyed many. But none were as monumental an experience as this first one.

CHAPTER TWO
SEEKING TO FIND MY LIFE'S PURPOSE

By Vicki Monroe

Your soul mission is your reason for being, your life purpose. It's your calling in life—who you feel called to be, what you feel called to do. Mission is an energy that flows through you—a drive, voice, or passion that you cannot ignore... It's what you know in your heart you must live if you are to experience inner peace and harmony.

~ Alan Seale

A few months after my first visit from Heather and Tom, I received news from home that my father was diagnosed with terminal bone cancer at the age of forty-nine. Bret put in for a transfer with the Air Force to relocate back home. Three months later, I was back in the United States. I would spend the next few years learning about a different kind of death experience. Unlike the sudden, unexpected, death of my sister, the death of my father was slow and painful.

These experiences with my father's and Heather's passing made me aware of my mortality. I began to wonder what purpose my life had. In fact, I had an overwhelming sense that I was supposed to be doing something, but I had no idea what that was. In the next few years, I had two more children, Bret and I built a house, and I went to nursing school. Then I began working at a nursing home.

THE NURSE

Working as a nurse in geriatrics wasn't what I expected. I loved working with the elderly, but I was immediately frustrated with the way some of the doctors and nurses treated the people who were dying. So many of these health care professionals were disconnected and insensitive. I understood that they did not have the privilege of my experiences with people in spirit, but they did not want to hear about them either. And when they saw me interacting with the dying and sometimes giving them messages from their awaiting loved ones in spirit—which always 'had a calming and comforting effect on each patient—I was either reprimanded or ridiculed.

After a great deal of aggravation wrestling with the status quo, I left nursing to escape the frustration of knowing my gift could comfort people but not being allowed to use it. If you remember the late 1980s and early 1990s, psychic mediums were not popular, there were no television shows where mediums demonstrated spirit communication with audience members, and most people didn't know the difference between a psychic and a medium. My ability to communicate with spirits was still not something of interest to most people, but rather, something strange and unusual with which most people didn't know what to believe when faced with it.

THE MECHANIC

Feeling the need to run away from it altogether, I searched for a vocation that was more physical and less metaphysical—I became a mechanic at an oil change and lube shop. I changed people's oil, rotated tires, and got grease under my fingernails. At first it was great. Aside from the girl at the front desk, I worked with a bunch of guys who couldn't care less about my otherworldly experiences. I knew this job change was a bit extreme, but unusual circumstances incite extreme measures. In hindsight, I was probably seeking to escape the conflicts that came with seeing and hearing spirits. And I guess I figured that this job was about as distant from it as I could get.

Funny thing about destiny, however, is that life doesn't just give us one chance to grab hold of it. If at first we miss an opportunity to fulfill our purpose in this lifetime, new possibilities will be right around the next bend. Needless to say, I turned that bend when I least expected it.

I was enjoying my new trade at the car repair shop, not thinking about spirits or the spirit world, when, all of a sudden, I got into a customer's car to do an oil change and there it was again! I instantly knew the car had been in an accident and that injuries had resulted. This was my psychic ability kicking in. A few days later, I heard a woman singing to me in the car shop's restroom. This wasn't too strange until I realized I was the only one in the bathroom, that is, the only one in physical form. Apparently the business was built on someone's home and this woman had been buried on the property. This was my spirit communication ability kicking in.

I finally realized there was no escaping the psychic mediumship, so after the novelty of working as a lube mechanic wore off, the inner void that had motivated me to go to nursing school and work at the nursing home took hold once again. I knew there was something I was supposed to be doing, yet I still had no idea what that was. You might wonder why it wasn't obvious to me that spirit communication was my calling. I simply never saw my ability to communicate with spirits as a career skill. I could not visualize using my gift in a job. And with so many people rejecting my claims to see and hear spirits, who would possibly pay me for it? There was just too much distance in my mind between this gift that I had learned to keep discreet and the void I sought to fill in my life. Although it seems obvious in hindsight, it wasn't at the time.

THE CARETAKER

So, once again, I took a job that I hoped would give me fulfillment. I loved horses, so I became caretaker of a three-hundred-year-old estate with functioning horse barn and horses. Once again, however, the moment I became comfortable there, I began learning the estate's history—first hand, that is. I began seeing spirits all over the place.

I saw Civil War soldiers, Revolutionary War soldiers, and a woman who was murdered by hanging in the barn. I also saw that there was once a fire there. Had I understood that there would be some meaning to it all—that this was simply practice for what was to come—I might have enjoyed these experiences more. Instead, the visions confused me. I didn't understand why I saw these things that no one else could see. And because people still looked at me cross-eyed when I talked about them, they were usually encounters that I kept to myself. As you might expect, this job, too, failed to cease the stirring in my heart that there was something I was supposed to be doing.

THE NATUROPATH

Because I had gone to nursing school and was always interested in holistic healing, I went back to school to become a naturopath. My studies in natural medicine immediately resonated with me like nothing else I had tried, so while going to school I traded my job at the horse barn for a position at a local health food store.

Studying holistic health care was fascinating to me, and talking to customers at the health food store about everything I was learning was most gratifying. I really felt like I was doing something that helped people. After getting my BS in naturology, I hung a shingle as a naturologist while continuing school for my doctorate degree. Everything seemed to be working as it should and I finally believed I knew where my life was going.

I wasn't allowed to give holistic health care advise as a store clerk, but the health food store owner allowed me to offer my naturology consulting services by putting a stack of my business cards on the counter. Now, anyone desiring to learn which vitamins, minerals, herbs and natural remedies could help them with their ailments and conditions could pay me for my knowledge. Within a few days, a store customer picked up my business card and called me for an appointment.

THE SPIRIT MESSENGER

When Elizabeth walked into my office, she was basically looking for nutritional advice. As we progressed with her evaluation, I first heard a slam on my desk that scared me a bit. Interestingly, it didn't seem to faze Elizabeth. Then I saw her grandmother—in spirit—who was attempting to get my attention by slamming her cane on my desk. She insisted I tell Elizabeth she was there. At first, I thought to myself, "Is this spirit talking to me?" Except for the spirits of friends and family, no spirit belonging to a *stranger* had ever spoken directly to me before; that is, not asking me to give someone I didn't know a message. I couldn't believe this was happening, and during my first naturology session, too! I was not excited about the timing of this new experience at all.

"No way," I thought to myself, "this is my first client. She's going to think I'm nuts."

I tried to ignore her, but Elizabeth's grandmother was adamant. "Tell her I'm here," she persisted, "she needs to know."

When it was obvious to me that she wasn't leaving (this is before I learned to draw boundaries with spirits), I asked Elizabeth if she had a grandmother who had passed. Then I proceeded to tell her that her grandmother was standing behind her and wanted her to know that she was with her. Elizabeth was open to the messages, which was a huge relief to me.

Elizabeth's naturology session went well, but it was the messages from her deceased grandmother that Elizabeth shared with her friends. Before I knew it, she was referring people to come see me—not for naturology, for which I spent years going to school—but for spirit communication, which came naturally to me. The irony was not lost on me.

Elizabeth referred a group of three people to me who shared a reading in order to split the one-hour fee. This was so new to me that I didn't know if any spirits would even show up, but I figured I didn't have to charge them if nothing happened. Spirits did show up, and I conveyed the messages they gave me for each client. One client's name was Derek, and he was especially moved by the reading. Then, within days, he referred his brother-in-law to me, a guy named Bob Olson.

THE READING THAT CHANGED TWO LIVES

Derek's brother-in-law, Bob Olson, called me up on a Sunday morning. He was very business-like, a "let's get to the point" kind of guy. I could tell by his voice that he was intrigued by what Derek had told him, but I got a sense that he wouldn't believe any messages I gave him. I remembered that Heather had told me that I was going to be challenged, and it was obvious to me that this would be one of those challenges.

Then another first occurred for me. I began getting spirit messages for Bob while I had him on the phone. Among other messages, I was being told it was important that I do this reading. At the time, I thought it was important for Bob, which it was; but I had no idea how important this reading was for me, as well. I set an appointment with Bob for four o'clock that day.

Still very new to this—as this was basically only my second reading appointment since three people shared my second appointment—I wondered all day how I should approach it. Again, I wondered if any spirits would come through. I knew Bob was the kind of guy who would want very precise messages or it wasn't going to fly. So I decided that I shouldn't ask him any questions and would have him answer only "yes, no or maybe" when asked if he understood the messages, thereby giving him no reason to think I was deducting information from his answers.

When Bob showed up for the appointment, my expectations were verified. He was the epitome of the word "skeptic." Worse, I could tell he was a cynic. His energy, his body language and his reserved conversation all screamed that he was testing me, big time! I felt like I was being interrogated by the FBI. It turns out that he was a former private investigator, so my feelings were not far from the truth. I knew I had my work cut out for me.

I'd like to say that Bob turned out being more open than I expected. The truth was, however, that he was extremely unforgiving and unrelenting in giving away anything in his words or body language, not even an expression that he was enjoying the reading. I couldn't even look at him at first because his expression was blank, except for a look that said, "I'm going to prove you are full of shit!"

About forty-five minutes to an hour into the reading, and after a multitude of evidential information, I started to see a glimmer of hope in Bob's eyes, a possibility of belief inside this guy. I started to see an auric light around him where darkness had resided. I knew this was a good sign that the reading was going well. When Bob's father, in spirit, told Bob he was especially proud of him while watching him play his saxophone solo in the middle school band concert, I noticed tears trickling down Bob's face. I jumped up from the couch and grabbed him a box of Kleenex. I could feel that this was going to be a reading that neither of us would ever forget. I never looked at the clock and just kept delivering the messages.

As I relayed the most specific and intimate messages from his father—apologies for his father's alcoholism, compassion for a chronic depression Bob had suffered, appreciation for the lilacs Bob's mother left on his grave—I began crying, too. The messages were so precise and meaningful that even I was deeply moved by what was coming through. I could feel the gravity of his father's love for him, as if Bob was my own son. Bob's reading was the first to teach me the depth and detail possible in a reading. And it taught me the power a reading has to transform someone's life. Witnessing Bob's reaction and change in aura, and his realization that there is much beyond the world as he had perceived it, gave me the confidence that my decision to keep the reading going was correct. It was like Bob was shedding an old coat and putting on a new one before walking out the door.

The reading went on for three hours. When it was over,

Bob's father said to me, "Expect something to happen." The next day Bob emailed me that he wanted to write his next book about his reading experience and my gift. That was in 1999. Neither of us knew it would take this long to get here. Neither of us knew what was ahead. It was the beginning of an incredible journey for both of us. One spirit messenger and one skeptic... well, former skeptic. I'll let Bob tell you about that in the next chapter.

CHAPTER THREE
THE SKEPTIC MEETS THE SPIRIT MESSENGER

By Bob Olson

It is the secret of the world that all things subsist and do not die, but only retire a little from sight and afterwards return again. Nothing is dead; men feign themselves dead, and endure mock funerals and mournful obituaries, and there they stand looking out of the window, sound and well, in some new strange disguise.

~ Ralph Waldo Emerson

On Friday the 15th of January, 1999, my newly published book was released. I'll admit it was exciting. However, a couple days after its release I had a talk with my father. That was a great deal more exciting because my father had been dead for almost two years. And this is where my story begins.

THE SKEPTIC

My wife, Melissa, and I were at her parents' summer home in Wells, Maine for a long weekend. The New England weather had been furious, biting cold with tankards of snow. Homeowners, business owners, and even the town highway departments could not contend with the persistent snowfall, so roads and driveways were spotted with icy-white glaciers where the snow had become petrified on the asphalt.

Because Melissa's brother, Derek, and I were both donning large bruises on our derrieres due to the icy driveway, we thought it wise to spread some sand before someone really got hurt. Living so close to the ocean, the beach seemed the obvious place to obtain a bucket of sand. Later we learned there are laws against such an act. Thinking about it in hindsight, that makes sense. But at the time, we were just two dumb cavemen finding a solution to our problem.

Derek had recently visited a nearby psychic medium, someone who communicates with spirits. So during our trip to the ocean, he enthusiastically narrated the amazing details she revealed about his life, "Information she could never have known," he exclaimed. "Things you and Melissa don't even know," he added for emphasis. The story lasted until the driveway was covered with sand. In the end, I was both intrigued and frostbitten.

Over the weekend, Derek's story dominated my thoughts the way a teenage boy thinks about sex, constantly yet silently. I was deeply skeptical, but I thought it was fun going to psychics and fortunetellers. Derek and I, as well as other members of Melissa's family, had gone to spiritual practitioners in the past. I was never impressed and thought every one of them to be a fraud. Nevertheless, I continued to try new ones for the entertainment of it and always with a spec of hope that I might find one with a genuine gift.

Because my curiosity teased me, I finally phoned Derek's psychic medium on the last day of our stay. Her name is Vicki Monroe. It was Sunday so I really didn't expect she would see me; but it was worth making the call because not knowing if she was legitimate was toying with my sanity. I was taken by surprise when she said I could come to her home at four o'clock that afternoon. I booked the appointment and hung up the phone.

I immediately regretted making the appointment. Melissa and I weren't rolling in greenbacks at the time, so I had a sense that I was wasting the money it was going to cost for the one-hour reading. I expected this Vicki Monroe woman was another fraud adept at firing off generalizations that could pertain to nearly everyone who walked through her door. It wasn't that I didn't believe Derek's story, but I saw him as a "believer"; and being a skeptic, I sometimes wondered if Derek was a bit naïve when it came to such matters. I considered calling Vicki back and canceling the appointment.

Melissa convinced me to not cancel, saying I originally wanted to go so it was important that I keep the appointment. She was confused by my sudden change of mind. I explained my skepticism and she replied by arousing my curiosity again: "What if she really is gifted? Derek said she was. You'll always wonder unless you go." I hesitated in thought. "Look," she said, "You already made the appointment, it would be rude to cancel now." She was right, of course. I made the decision to go.

The weather that January day had a suspicious change of mood, an April sun with an air of rebirth in the breeze and melting ice. After a refreshing day by the ocean, Melissa and I made the trip to Vicki's home. As we made the half-hour drive into the countryside, swerving to dodge the ice chunks that hated my Volvo, I vowed not to divulge a single hint about my personality, my work, my marriage, my family, my past or my future goals during conversation with Vicki. "If this woman is truly gifted, she is going to have to prove it," I demanded. We even decided that Melissa would stay in the car so that Vicki couldn't visually learn anything about Melissa or deduct any revealing signals about our relationship. I was putting this so-called psychic medium to the test and she was going to have to earn her money without any help from me.

THE SPIRIT MESSENGER

As we drove up the endless gravel driveway, Melissa and I were instantly drenched with envy at the view of Vicki's postcard farmhouse with an operational barn, horses roaming the fields and children sledding in the snow a short distance away. I avoided the chickens and parked our car so nobody in the house could see Melissa. As I approached the doorway, I met with memories of my past as I heard the children's voices echo across the snow-glazed fields. I knocked and was immediately greeted by a woman I assumed to be Vicki.

I couldn't really see her, as the sun was beaming and the front porch entryway was shadowed. She invited me in and I followed her to an in-law apartment attached to the farmhouse. She said it was where her mother lived, but that her mother was away on vacation. It was spacious and clean with that new addition feel to it, and it was furnished with comfortable cozy chairs and a couch. I quickly sat on the first chair I approached as if to seek sanctuary from my fears and uncertainty, trying not to expose my jittery limbs. Finally, I got a look at Vicki.

I was expecting a slightly rotund forty-or-fifty-something-year-old woman wearing a gypsy outfit and sporting a rather large wart on her face. Instead, Vicki was a thin, small-framed thirty-something-year-old, no wart, and wore white jeans and a fleece top. Except for her flaming red locks that fell past her shoulders and framed her entire face—giving her a witches-of-Salem kind of look—she appeared very normal.

My immediate impression was that she was way too

young and much too pretty to be a "real" psychic medium. All I could think was, "I might as well just give her my money and leave. This is going to be a complete waste of time." I figured Vicki read a couple books on developing your psychic abilities or spirit communication and decided it was a good way to make extra cash while she stayed at home with the kids. Now that I saw her and sized her up, I could feel my body language change from hopefully anxious to skeptically aloof.

Since I quickly snapped up the chair, Vicki walked to my left and sat on the couch, rather comfortably I noticed, with her legs bent under her like she was about to watch a movie with the family. I half expected the microwave to ding signaling the popcorn was ready. Her casualness made me feel a tiny bit at ease, but I knew even she sensed my guard was still up. She told me that she didn't want me to tell her anything about myself, and only to answer her questions with a "yes, no or maybe." She didn't want me to add any details or fill-in with information that she was missing, because she would eventually put it all together as the reading progressed.

I had already vowed (to Melissa and myself) not to tell her anything, but I was now more relaxed knowing she wasn't going to pry. My curiosity was peaked. All I could think was, "What if she's legit?" And then I quickly caught hold of myself, remembering all the phony psychics and fortunetellers I had visited in the past. I was determined not to let my guard down and get suckered in by her calm-mannered unassuming manipulation.

READING THE BOOK OF MY LIFE

Within minutes, Vicki was rattling off details about my life that were hard to chalk up to a lucky guess. She told me that she communicates with people's spirit-guides, "angels if you prefer to call them, but without the wings," she said. These are spirits, souls, who are "in the light," and are around each of us to help aid us through life. She said we all have many guides who help us with the different facets of our existence. Some are people we know from this lifetime who have passed on and have made the transition back to the spirit world. Others are souls who did not exist in this lifetime but have been with us in other lifetimes, or at least have been with us in the spirit world between lives.

Vicki talked like a poet. She had this calming tone to her voice where her words flowed from her lips like a violin playing Mozart. I thought to myself how she would be perfect for one of those meditation tapes. But it was more than the sound of her voice; it was also the words she chose, melodically lyrical, bordering on angelic (if you'll excuse the pun). Yet it didn't sound phony like someone repeating a poem that they don't really understand. Vicki's words came from her heart. And, slowly, they melted my icy apprehension. I couldn't help but to stop fighting her like a cat in a net and at least listen to what she was saying.

Vicki said that the spirit world is actually "home" to us. I thought this was a comforting notion. "This earthly existence is a temporary place of learning and growing," she said.

"Much like college?" I jumped in.

"Sure. A little bit like going away to school," she patiently replied. Vicki explained that, when we die, our souls leave this earthly life of fleshly confinement to go home where we feel free and liberated in the surrounding comfort of God's light and love.

As nice as it sounded, a lot of this went right over my head like so much mumbo-jumbo. I was somewhat ignorant in this area. And while it was all amusingly interesting to me, I also didn't know what to make of it. I was still skeptical and was not going to be made the fool. Then she told me that two of my guides were in the room.

"Huh?..."

I took a deep breath. She identified them as my grandmother (whom she identified by name) and my father (whom she described with accuracy). It was lucky for Vicki that both had died, I thought. How embarrassing it would have been if they were still alive. But they weren't. Okay, she got lucky. I waited for more evidence.

Vicki said that my grandmother was telling her that I was a big skeptic, a "wanna-believer" who hoped there was an afterlife but needed a lot of proof. "Bingo" on the latter. She told Vicki that they needed to prove to me that my grandmother was really there. She proceeded to name a few of my cousins by their first names. Not bad considering the names she gave were all my grandmother's grandchildren. She also congratulated me on my new business venture.

Vicki told me that my grandmother was placing white flowers all around me. With this, and the "energy-feeling" Vicki received along with the white flower visual, it was a symbol to Vicki of congratulations relating to something of a business nature, as opposed to a birth or a marriage which would likely be different colored flowers or a different energy-feeling that came with the flower symbol.

I suspected that the congratulations were related to the fact that my new book had been released a couple days prior, but there was no way I was going to give that information to Vicki. Without any hints from me, she eventually did figure out that not only was I having a book published, but also that the book was about a grueling time in my life that involved unfathomable suffering (the book is about my experience during a five-year chronic depression). Since Vicki can also sense the emotion the spirits are feeling, tears rolled down her face as my guides expressed their love and sorrow for me during that five-year struggle. I must confess that I was quite taken by Vicki's willingness to become so emotionally involved for my benefit.

LIFTING THE VEIL

There are several ways that spirits communicate with Vicki. The first is by allowing her to observe them visually. The second is simply through verbal communication. The only problem with this is that not everything comes through with clarity. It's like listening to an AM radio station with static. A third means of communication is through the use of symbolic messages where pictures or words are placed in Vicki's mind telepathically. The fourth way that Vicki receives messages from the spirit world is through sensations in her body. For instance, if a spirit wants Vicki to know that they died from pneumonia but they can't describe it verbally, Vicki might feel pressure in her lungs and a sensation of suffocation. If they want her to get the message of fear or love, they can cause her to feel either of those emotions or any emotion they need to convey.

But I'm getting ahead of myself. It's hard not to considering my one-hour reading lasted over three hours. Yes, that was interesting, because once the reading got rolling and I knew for sure that I was communicating with my deceased grandmother and father, I couldn't just say, "Sorry Vicki, sorry Dad, sorry Gram, but I really can't afford to talk anymore, so...see ya' later." Once the skepticism has been demolished with undeniable evidence, money really doesn't matter at a time like that. I had no choice. I had to keep going.

And keep going I did, as I mentioned, for three gut-wrenching hours. Vicki wasn't the only one with tears in her eyes that evening. I bathed in my own tears more than once. I cried when my father apologized through Vicki for what his alcoholism did to our family. I cried when my father told me that one of his proudest moments was watching me play a solo on my saxophone during the middle school band concert. I cried when my father told me to thank my mother for the lilacs she left on his grave (lilacs were his favorite flower). And I cried when my father described the scene at the hospital as he died from lung cancer.

The conversation transported me back to that vivid memory: my mother, my sister, Melissa and I surrounding my father's hospital bed and holding him tightly as the doctor removed the breathing tube. For ten minutes, but more like an eternity, we watched as he took his last few breaths. We listened as the monitors signaled his vital signs with an emotionless beeping that slowed in rhythm as his soul escaped the confines of his cancerous flesh. When my mother twice burst into a panicked wailing of tears at the realization that her life-long best friend was leaving her forever, the monitor's beeping escalated as if to say, "I'm sorry honey, I will try to stay for you a little longer." Upon realizing how difficult her crying was making it for him, my mother gained control of herself and the beeping slowed once again. Then she did this two more times, and my father attempted to hang on with each fit of tears. After my mother calmed down, my father's face lost all color and then turned a grayish blue. His chest, previously the only evidence of life and movement, became motionless. And when that hidden source of energy, that which we call life, had obviously left his worn-out body, Mom hugged Dad one last time like she was never going to let him go. At the age of fifty-nine, my mother had become a lonely widow.

Hearing Vicki communicate my father's words to me was a gift beyond monetary value. My mouth was silent, but my eyes spoke chapters as tears of happiness and love journeyed from my heart to my cheeks. She relayed to me my own thoughts, the exact words of my prayers that my father had heard and was now repeating back to me. He even suggested an occasional frustration with me for not acknowledging his presence when I surely knew he was with me. To not weep, to not become wholeheartedly enveloped within my memories of him, I would have had to be dead myself. The experience was so much more than poignant; it was a moment engraved in time.

ALL IN THE FAMILY

After two emotional hours, and in a moment of realization, I remembered Melissa was waiting in the car. Being that it was January in New England, the sun goes down by 4:30 p.m. and the frigid cold returns even on the sunniest of days. It was about 6:00 p.m. when I suddenly looked at my watch. Vicki must have been confused when, panic stricken, my eyes widened and I jumped from my seat.

"Oh my God, my wife is waiting in the car. Can I get her? Will this disrupt the reading? My father and grandmother won't go away will they?"

Vicki assured me that there would be no disruption, and she was immediately concerned about Melissa. To my surprise, I ran out to the car but it was empty. Confused, I went back into the house. When I saw one of Vicki's children, I asked if he had seen Melissa. Apparently, Vicki's husband, Bret, had kindly invited Melissa out of the cold car to join him and their four children in the warm house. Bret and Melissa were having a nice visit when I interrupted to have her join the reading. Melissa had no idea what she was about to experience.

Vicki and I quickly gave Melissa the Reader's Digest version of what had occurred so far in the reading. We told her who was present in the room and mentioned a few snippets of information that related specifically to her; for one, that my father had instructed me to thank her for the candles she lights every morning upon waking me up. He said he loved the "ambiance" of the candles. Then he joked, "Imagine me using a word like 'ambiance?'" It was true; my father had the look of a ruggedly handsome movie star but the vernacular of a truck driver. For him to use a word like ambiance would have sounded funny. We all laughed at my father's modesty. It was typical of his character to make fun of himself.

Secondly, my father wanted me to inform Melissa that he particularly likes the *vanilla* candles that she frequently burns. With that said, and within only moments of her arrival, Melissa had tears trickling down her cheeks and into the corners of her mouth. Either her protective wall of skepticism wasn't as rock-solid as my own, thereby not requiring an hour of unmitigated evidence to tear it down, or she trusted my assertion that Vicki's gift was real when I hurriedly explained the situation to her while leading her from Bret's company to the in-law apartment where Vicki waited. Regardless, Melissa was quick to understand that she was witnessing an event that would forever change both my life and her own. And she was understandably sentimental about our reunion with my father whom she had known since she was just twelve years old, when we first began dating.

After the third hour, which included additional messages from both Melissa's guides and my own, Vicki's energy was observably spent. Still, it was equally obvious that the reading was as gratifying for her as it was life-changing for us. No one wanted the night to end and we continued to talk for about an hour, mostly with Vicki enlightening us as we fired off the multitude of questions that had exploded in our thoughts during the reading. Eventually, it was time to go. It was eight o'clock on a Sunday night and Vicki's children had not eaten, although Bret saved the day by arriving with pizza as we said our goodbyes.

The two-hour ride home was unusually quiet as Melissa and I pondered the dreamlike events of the last few hours. Melissa broke the silence by admitting she was "feeling a little creeped-out," not sure she would ever feel comfortable again while getting undressed. "Who knows who might be watching?" she joked with a touch of concern in her voice. I assured her that any spirits around us would surely be polite enough not to look, and that issues of the flesh were not likely to have any effect on them in the spirit world anyway. I think my words comforted her, but now she had me thinking about it. As I continued to contemplate the reading, it was evident that this insightful milestone was triggering more questions than it had answered. And all the way home, and all during that sleepless night, my mind kept returning to one assertive thought: "This is the beginning to an incredible book!"

PART II
Understanding Skepticism

CHAPTER FOUR
TALKED TO ANY DEAD PEOPLE LATELY?

By Bob Olson

The reasonable man adapts himself to the world; the unreasonable one persists in trying to adapt the world to himself. Therefore, all progress depends on the unreasonable man.

~ *George Bernard Shaw*

The day after my reading with Vicki, I drove Melissa to work and did my best impression of Mario Andretti (a race car driver) on the way back home. I sprinted into my office and dialed up my friend David to tell him the news of the prior evening's activities.

Interestingly, laying news of this nature on somebody, even one of your best friends, is not something for which we become prepared in the course of normal everyday events. How was I going to bring up *this* subject? "Hi Dave, talked to any dead people lately? I have!" Nonetheless, after the initial small talk about weather and work, I blurted it out.

Well, blurted might be an exaggeration; stumbled is a better description. The first thing I found myself doing was setting the whole story up before presenting it. "Now, David, you might think my cheese has finally slid off my cracker, but

I assure you that what I'm about to tell you is true." Inevitably, I wrestled my way through the appetizer and moved on to the meat and potatoes.

LISTING THE EVIDENCE

David accepted the tale like a true friend. "Wow, that *is* a lot to take in, Bob. If it were coming from anybody else, I'd never believe it." There was a long pause. "Phoebe is gonna *freak* when she hears this story. Tell me more, tell me more" (Phoebe is David's wife).

It helps to know that David is a computer guy. I really don't know his exact title, but he works with computers, so he's basically a left-brain personality. In other words, for him to accept this, he really had to hear some evidence. And I was prepared to give him *all* the details.

You see, to me—at this early stage of my adventure into mediumship—the *details* of my reading were all the evidence anyone could possibly require. With a three-hour reading, I had pages of details that I had written down while Vicki talked. As far as I was concerned, I had the equivalent of scientific proof (so I thought). But as I began presenting it to David, I quickly learned that "proof" is subjective when it comes to matters of spirituality; and to *really* affect one's beliefs, the evidence must come from *personal* experience.

I told David how my father and grandmother had given me numerous names of people in my life, far too many to call it lucky. Vicki even mentioned David's daughter's name, *Daisy*. (People love to know when they're included in a reading. It always grabs their attention.) She also gave me the names: Carol (my mother), Melissa (my wife), Kris (my friend), Kristen (my friend), Jamie (my friend), John (my friend), Emily (my aunt), Steve (my cousin), Pam (my cousin / Steve's sister), Mary (my grandmother), Joseph (my grandfather), Scott (my brother-in-law)… and *Brian*, who Vicki described as, "a cousin who is more like a brother to you." Brian was a younger cousin of mine who came to live with my family after his parents died in a plane crash.

Vicki was aware that my cousin, Brian, was ten-years-old when both his parents died in that plane accident. Brian's mother is the "Emily" mentioned in the list of names my grandmother gave me. Neither Vicki nor I knew why, but Emily presided quietly at my reading holding a white handkerchief in her right hand. For their children's sake, Brian's parents had always traveled separately for fear that such a tragedy would occur. Somehow they must have known the plane crash was in their life blueprints. Brian's grandmother passed away without warning and his parents were forced to fly together from Alabama to Massachusetts in order to arrive on time for the funeral service. That one exception to their rule resulted in one funeral service for all three people—his parents *and* his grandmother. Brian came to live with us after that tragic event and became part of my family. I was thirteen years old.

I continued to tell David how my grandmother and father were both pleading with me during the reading to attempt contact with Brian because we had lost touch with one another over the years. It was the most recurring theme of my reading. My father, through Vicki, also told me where Brian lived, where he worked, how many children he had, as well as additional, yet more personal, details about his life. Everything Vicki said was correct.

David listened with attentive ears and wanted to know everything. I continued to explain how Vicki knew, from my father's communication, that my mother was considering doing volunteer work and that Melissa and I were considering getting a dog. She even knew that we specifically wanted a yellow Labrador. She then added, with uncanny accuracy, that Melissa wanted a yellow Lab and I wanted a chocolate one; but I had decided upon yellow because I wanted to please Melissa. I told David how remarkable this all was, especially considering I had just purchased a Labrador calendar for my office a couple days prior.

Except for an occasional comment where David used the word "holy" emphasized with some cursing, he sat in pensive silence, now letting his voicemail system accept all his phone calls. I continued my story by explaining how Vicki proved to me that my father is always with me. He described precisely what my home looked like regarding the furniture and its placement in certain rooms. He also mysteriously gave a play-by-play narrative of our normal routine inside our home: how I wrote in my office every evening while Melissa cooked dinner in the kitchen and listened to the news from our mini-television on the counter; and how we read in bed every night with me beside the window to my right and Melissa to my left in the corner.

Vicki knew we owned a second vehicle, a four-wheel drive SRV. She knew of my sister's divorce and the traits of her personality. She knew my father loved car shows and baseball, as well as the television shows *MASH* and *All In The Family*. She knew about Melissa's two sisters and described their personalities like she had known them for years. She knew that Melissa and I dreamed of moving to Maine. She knew about my parents' miscarriage. Vicki appeared to know more about Melissa and myself than we knew about each other; and we had been together since she was twelve and I was fifteen, about twenty years prior to this reading.

THE SHOE'S ON THE OTHER FOOT

David couldn't wait to tell Phoebe the story. His enthusiasm oozed from his pores. But he confessed that it was all very difficult for him to accept. "I hear you telling me all this, Bob, and I believe you—I really do—but there is a part of me that refuses to accept it. It's like, I know you're not pulling a prank on me, but I'm waiting for you to start laughing and yell 'Gotcha!'"

David acknowledged that he would have to find out for himself, and go see Vicki on his own. The following day he called me back saying, "You've gotta call Phoebe and tell her that story. I just can't tell it like you do, even though I took notes while you told me about it. She thought it was interesting, but she's having a hard time believing it. You have to call her, Bob. She'll believe it if *you* tell her the story."

I did call Phoebe to tell her the story, but now the shoe was on the other foot. I finally knew how Derek must have felt when telling me *his* story. And thus I learned the first lesson of spiritual experiences: belief comes from personal, not vicarious, experience. If there is even an ounce of skepticism, as there is in most people, individuals need to experience such things personally in order to overcome that doubt. One cannot overcome it by hearing about *other* people's experiences. This is why I recommend that anyone interested in such matters have a personal reading with a genuine and legitimate psychic medium. All the reading you could ever do on this subject will never take the place of this divine, life-altering, experience.

CHAPTER FIVE
SKEPTICISM FROM A PSYCHIC MEDIUM'S SIBLINGS

By Bob Olson

There are more things in heaven and earth, Horatio,
Than are dreamt of in your philosophy.

~ Hamlet

Now that I understood the concept that *"believing* comes from personal, not vicarious, experience" this theory was further confirmed to me while interviewing Vicki's sister and two brothers for this book. I apparently didn't fully understand the necessity for having a personal experience because my interviews with Vicki's siblings caught me totally by surprise when I sensed some skepticism in their answers.

NEEDING MORE PROOF

The first interview that really threw me for a loop was with Amy Jo Hansen, Vicki's sister. Arrogantly, I expected to know the answers Amy would provide before I interviewed her. I assumed that Amy would obligingly defend Vicki's gift for the mere fact that they were sisters. Boy, was I wrong.

The best description I can give for Amy's position regarding Vicki's abilities is that she was *skeptically supportive.*

Amy told me, "I want to believe this is one-hundred percent true, but I want proof that this is really happening. Vicki knows me so well; how will I ever know if it is coming from *over there* or coming from Vicki's subconscious memories?" she concluded.

I was floored by the interview! I hung up the phone and ran to Melissa, "How can it be that her own sister is skeptical?" I questioned. "Amy told me about casual readings where Vicki gave her detailed information that she believed Vicki *could not* have known. Yet, she still wonders if Vicki could have heard it from somebody else in the family. Her refusal to get past her skepticism puzzles me," I told Melissa (how quick I was to forget what it's like to be a skeptic). It wasn't until I interviewed Vicki's brothers that the lesson regarding "personal versus vicarious experiences" was *truly* confirmed, and finally sank into my thick skull.

I BELIEVE THAT SHE BELIEVES IT

"Do you believe Vicki is spiritually gifted?" I asked David Chadbourne, Vicki's younger brother.

"Who am I to question it?" he answered. "Vicki's an honest person. I don't see why I should doubt it," he added, leaving me hanging unsatisfied with his impreciseness. Even when I called him on his ambiguous answer, he was unable to come right out and say what I had originally expected from him, "Of course I believe she communicates with spirits. She's my sister, damn it!" Instead I got, "If she believes it, who am I to argue?" Frankly, I was frustrated by his answer, feeling he was dodging the question. But the truth is he was being totally honest with me. It was *I* who was refusing to recognize the lesson in his honesty.

ON THE OUTSIDE CURIOUS ABOUT THE INSIDE

Vicki's older brother, Chuck Chadbourne, was more straightforward, although still not what I had expected from a psychic medium's sibling. "I'm a skeptical believer. That's a polite way of putting it," he confessed. "I'm looking from the outside, curious about what it's like on the inside," he embellished, catching me off guard that this "let's get to the point" kind-of-guy used a metaphor. I had to ask Chuck to pause for a moment so I could think about what he said. Then he continued, "While I have a hard time believing we can talk to dead people, I admit I'm uneducated in this area. But I've watched some television specials about it, I'm currently reading James Van Praagh's book, and I have a lot respect for what he and Vicki do for people," Chuck admitted.

The interviews with Amy, David and Chuck started a debate inside my head. Was there something I had overlooked, something they knew that I had missed? If *they* aren't fully convinced that their own sister can talk with spirits, who am *I* to come to that conclusion? And in a tizzy of cerebral confusion and chaos, fear of public humiliation and ten-months of wasted research flooded my senses. My legs grew weak. My palms sweltered. I stood frozen—for three seconds or three hours, I'm not sure.

Then it hit me like a bug to a bumper. It wasn't *I* who was missing something. It was Amy, David and Chuck who's relationships and history with Vicki prevented them from sharing that experience I underwent on January 17, 1999— when Vicki, the perfect stranger, announced three hours of precious secrets from, and about, my most beloved family members and about my life. My panic transformed to sadness for their loss. I thought it unfortunate having such a gifted sister and never being able to benefit or enjoy the unworldly abilities she bestows.

All three siblings accredited their remaining skepticism to one obstacle: Vicki already knew everything about them. How could they know if the messages she retrieved from the spirit world were genuine while knowing she already held that knowledge in her memory bank? As a result, and because he became so intrigued by my enthusiasm for Vicki's gift, Chuck wanted to set up a reading for his secretary—a woman he knew well, but whom Vicki had never met. He hoped this scenario would be the next best thing to getting a personal reading and giving him the proof necessary to become a believer. So far, as I write this chapter, this little test hasn't transpired.

A FAMILY OF OTHERWORLDLY EXPERIENCES

What I find most interesting about all this is the fact that Vicki is not the only person in the family to have had otherworldly experiences. Amy has benefited from dreams where her father has visited her offering reassurance that her life is on-track, usually telling her to stop worrying. "That's my thing, self-doubt and worrying," Amy disclosed. "The next day after these dreams, I always feel a lot better. It's comforting," she explained.

David didn't want to talk about his experiences, but said it was okay to mention them in this book if other family members told me about them. Well, his mother, Nancy Chadbourne, tells the poignant account of the time David saw his sister, Heather, and Heather's husband, Tom, standing on either side of their gravesite at their funeral service—they were buried together after a tragic car accident that took their lives, as described by Vicki in Chapter One.

"David saw them standing beside the gravesite smiling

and looking at the rest of us. Tom was in his brown suit, and Heather wore her white dress," Nancy illustrated.

"Did you see them?" David asked Nancy after the service.

"No," Nancy replied, after asking David who he was talking about.

"Well, I did, but don't tell anyone because they'll think I'm crazy," pleaded David.

"Don't worry, I won't tell anyone," his mother said. Of course, that was over a decade ago, and David is used to his mother telling the story now. He just isn't comfortable talking about it himself. At least if someone hearing the story accuses him of being delusional, he can reply, "Hey, I didn't say that. That's just my mother telling stories again."

Chuck, too, acknowledged his share in the family oddities. First, he told me about the night after his sister, Heather, died. He and his wife Linda were staying over at Vicki and Bret's home in Germany for a visit. "I was emotional," he said, "So Linda was comforting me until I fell asleep. When I woke up in the middle of the night, Linda was totally out. I mean, I could have done anything in that living room where we were sleeping and I wouldn't have woken her up. I also noticed that the cuckoo clock had stopped. I got up and looked around the living room and saw Tom [Heather's husband] standing there in his infamous poncho and sneakers. I said, 'Tom, what the hell happened?" And Tom said, 'Don't worry about it, Chuck, we are fine. It's amazing here.' I asked Tom, 'Why the car accident?' And he said, 'We didn't feel a thing.' I just responded by saying, 'Okay,' and I went back to bed like I was going to see him again the next day."

"I don't think it was a dream," said Chuck, "I was focusing on too many things, like noticing the clock wasn't working. I actually tried to wake Linda up while Tom was there, and Tom smiled like he knew she wouldn't wake up. It was pretty cool, cause I had this feeling of peace afterward like they were okay."

Chuck also revealed a second incident he had experienced. "I had a more recent experience a couple years ago," he began. "I was driving, and I was really tired and beat, at risk of falling asleep. All of a sudden I had this overwhelming smell of perfume in the car. It was nasty. It was so strong. I opened the windows even though it was cold, but the smell wouldn't go away. The smell grew so powerful that I had to get out of my car. I mean, it stunk bad. So I stopped at a Burger King for a coffee. When I got back into my car, the smell was gone. Some people think it was Heather trying to get me to stop, maybe to get a coffee so I would wake up for safety's sake. I don't know about that. All I know is what happened," Chuck concluded.

Considering these unusual circumstances, especially where Chuck and David have seen spirits themselves, it is difficult for me to understand how skepticism could be in their vocabulary. However, Chuck still argues (with himself) that his conversation with Tom might have been a dream. And David won't even go there—he still won't tell the story even though he knows I've already heard it from his mother. So I realize, if they can't come to terms with their *own* experiences, it's only natural to expect them to have some doubt when it comes to Vicki's.

As a person who was once cynically skeptical, I think I understand where Amy, David and Chuck may be coming from. I really can't accuse any of them as being nonbelievers. David said he believed people could communicate with spirits long before Vicki had realized her gift. He has also come to terms with his own highly intuitive ability—he often knows what people are going to say before they say it. "In college, I used to have conversations with teammates and friends knowing word-for-word what they were going to say, and I just waited for them to say it. It still happens," he told me. "It just occurred the other day with a coworker. It's kind of cool, but it's just something that happens, " he explained.

Amy is a lot like I used to be, a "wanna believer" who just needs to be slapped in the face with undeniable evidence. She's also somewhat fearful of the paranormal. "I would like to have a formal reading with Vicki [as opposed to the casual happenstance readings at family gatherings], but I'm a little hesitant and a little nervous about what I might find out," she admitted. Later in the interview she repeated her fears: "I'm a little afraid of what I might find out. What if I learn I'm not going in the right direction with my life? That would be troubling to me," she said.

Now that I look closer at my interview with Amy, I'm not sure why I was so surprised of her remaining skepticism. Blood may be thicker than water, but when it comes to the supernatural, fear and skepticism will always question evidence if there is *any* possibility for deception—even when a trusted relative is providing the information. If Amy can face her fears, she may have to hire a psychic medium who knows absolutely nothing about her to become a believer. I doubt I would have crossed that line from skeptic to believer if Vicki were not a perfect stranger to *me* at the time of my first reading.

Chuck is the kind of guy who knows what he's experienced, and he's not afraid to talk about it. But he's also not willing to come to any conclusions, admitting that he's simply too uneducated in this field to really understand any of it. He's also too busy with work and other interests to take the time to think about metaphysical principles. There is a large population of society, including Chuck, that has little-to-no interest in communicating with the dead; and there's nothing wrong with that. I'm impressed that Chuck even took the time to read a book and watch some television specials on the subject. Understanding this about Chuck, it is not surprising that he never set up that reading for his secretary.

I interviewed Amy, David and Chuck only ten months into my four-year research of mediumship. I'm sure they have come a long way in their beliefs since those interviews. For one, Vicki is in the media constantly, gives public demonstrations to hundreds of people several times a year, and has been featured in several newspapers, magazines and television shows across the country. I'm sure Amy, David and Chuck have had much more experience with Vicki's gift today. But I'm glad I caught them at such an early stage, or I might not have learned the important lesson they taught me.

SPIRITUAL GROWTH COMES FROM PERSONAL, NOT VICARIOUS, EXPERIENCE

So what did I conclude based on these interviews? I determined that if Vicki's own family members were unable to make that leap of faith that her gift is real—solely because their history with her prevents them from having their own indisputable personal readings to prove it—then it is understandable why the rest of us doubters will require a personal experience of our own to overcome our skepticism to the point of becoming believers. Just like my friend David said, "I hear you telling me all this, Bob, and I believe you—I really do—but there is a part of me that refuses to accept it. It's like, I know you're not pulling a prank on me, but I'm waiting for you to start laughing and yell 'Gotcha!'"

In the end, all I can say is when your deceased father or

mother or your late Uncle Charlie starts telling you things—through a spirit messenger—that no other living soul knows, there's a paradigm shift in your belief structure, and what was once a string of unanswered questions now becomes a knowing. I have realized that a vicarious experience isn't really an experience at all; it is a fantasy, a story in our imagination that we heard from somebody else. But a personal experience is just that, an experience. It's a memory of an occurrence, a happening, an encounter—with all the emotions and bodily sensations that followed—that has become a part of our cellular makeup. It is more than just an experience in our memory; it is now a part of us. It is now who we are. And that is what spiritual growth is all about.

CHAPTER SIX
A SPIRIT MESSENGER'S TRIALS WITH SKEPTICISM

By Vicki Monroe

It is a profound mistake to think that everything has been discovered; as well think the horizon to be the boundary of the world.

~ *Antoine Marin Lemierre*

At this early stage in my work as a spirit messenger, the number of readings I was doing was still fairly sparse, certainly not enough to work at it full-time. Although the word-of-mouth referrals for my readings were growing, I booked most of my readings on weekends while juggling my time during the week as a health food store clerk, a mother of four and a student working towards her doctorate degree.

While my reputation as a spirit messenger grew slowly, my lessons as a spirit messenger came more rapidly. I quickly learned that my adulthood experiences would not be all that different from my childhood experiences. Some people did not believe I could communicate with spirits, thereby assuming I was a liar, or worse, a charlatan. Others did not understand what I did, and therefore, were fearful of it. And, still, others *mis*-understood it, and because it seemed to conflict with their religious beliefs, thought my gift surely must originate from evil.

THE MANY FACES OF SKEPTICISM

Basically, I characterize all these perceptions of my abilities under the category of skepticism. Webster's dictionary defines a *"skeptic"* as *"a person who questions the validity, authenticity, or truth of something purporting to be factual."* I have dealt with all sorts of skeptics. There are those who want to believe there is more to this world than what we perceive, but simply need more evidence to cross that bridge. There are those who want to believe, but are stuck on what they were taught by others. There are those who want to believe, but are extremely fearful of getting ripped off, appearing stupid or being made the fool. And there are those who only see things in black or white, and don't allow any room for possibilities outside their beliefs.

Skepticism is healthy unless it closes your mind to new possibilities. We should all be leery when someone claims to have abilities that extend beyond what we know to be possible. But, then, there was a time when we didn't think the world was round; we didn't think humans could run a mile in under four minutes; and we didn't think we could ever travel to the moon! Yet if we never allowed for new possibilities, where would we be today? People might still be afraid to sail to new frontiers for fear that we would fall off the edge of the earth.

Skepticism is healthy when it protects us from con artists who want us to believe in their scams. I wish *more* people had been skeptical of that psychic on television with the phony Jamaican accent. Her little act not only hurt a lot of people, it made it all the more difficult for legitimate psychic mediums in this country to use their gift for good. It is a sad fact, but there are a lot of charlatans in this business. People need to be skeptical to protect themselves. But don't let that shut you off from seeking genuinely gifted people who have much to offer. It doesn't hurt to allow yourself a little vulnerability. Just don't compromise anything you can't afford to lose, like cleaning out your bank account to have an evil spell removed. Take my word for it; there are no evil spells that need to be removed—period!

Most skeptics are very intelligent because they analyze everything. It's important to look at all sides of an issue before making any conclusions. But a healthy skepticism also allows for new discoveries. Our beliefs and thoughts are supposed to change throughout life. That is how we learn and grow. That is the natural flow of things. It is how wisdom is attained. We might learn that Santa is imaginary, and we might learn that spirits are not.

Then there is the hardcore, rigid skeptic. This type of skeptic is not analyzing anything. He is stuck in his beliefs and only seeks evidence that his beliefs are correct. When you try to prove how something is false, you miss evidence that it is true, and vice versa. Hardcore skeptics aren't really skeptics at all if we believe Webster's version that a skeptic "questions the validity, authenticity, or truth of something purporting to be factual." Hardcore skeptics are not "questioning" anything; they have already made up their minds. Hardcore skeptics are simply lining up evidence for what they believe. But evidence is not proof. I can line up plenty of evidence that Santa exists.

Interestingly, you might think that this book is an attempt to prove to you that what I do is real, or at least, that life-after-death is real. No book is going to do that for you. Bob and I have only written this book to introduce you to our individual journeys, with the intention that it might create a curiosity within you to investigate—analyze—this subject more. Curiosity is the first step. There are so many directions you can go from there.

In the end, I believe skepticism results from a lack of understanding my ability to communicate with spirits. As we know, a lack of understanding among differing ethnic groups, cultures and lifestyles can lead to prejudice, racism and hatred. This is all due to the *fear* that grows from such a lack of understanding. So, too, does a lack of understanding my abilities lead to fear and negative reactions. Since "I" know what I do is real—and I know that if everyone truly understood it the way I do, there wouldn't be any skeptics—I see this lack of understanding as the basis of skepticism.

Having said all this about skepticism, I'd like to give you a glimpse of what it's like to deal with skepticism from my perspective as a spirit messenger. Of all the hurdles a medium must go through in their life, I believe that dealing with skepticism, in its many forms, is one of the greatest challenges. And as you will notice, it isn't always easy, but it certainly keeps life interesting.

SKEPTICISM AND STRANGERS

One of my first "interesting" experiences came while I was still working at the health food store. A regular customer began coming in much more frequently than normal and he wanted to talk with me a lot. At first my coworker thought this guy had a little crush on me. That might have been easier to handle. Instead, after revealing to me that he was heavily medicated due to a mental illness causing him hallucinations, he confessed that he thought I could control his future with my "powers." He never fully explained if this was a belief or a hallucination, but I assumed it was simply based on a lack of insight regarding my abilities.

In spite of every effort to convince him that I have no

ability to affect anyone's future but my own—a little thing called freewill—he slowly escalated from constant customer to scary stalker. The day I looked out a window of my home and found him standing on my front lawn in the middle of a lightning storm was the day I realized I had a serious problem. The problem wasn't resolved immediately, but with the help of police it finally stopped.

My husband, Bret, already had concerns with how people might react to my "coming out" as a spirit messenger, so this incident only added fuel to his fears. I was giving readings at my house because there weren't enough clients to warrant an office, so this added a grocery list of concerns for Bret. "You're inviting people that we know nothing about into our home. And now I don't have to tell you that some of the people you may attract might not be mentally stable. Perhaps this isn't such a great idea," Bret reasoned.

Unfortunately for Bret, giving up my readings was not an option for me. After years of searching, I now knew at the very core of my being what I was supposed to be doing with my life. I found purpose in my life, which finally filled the void that had tormented me for so long. I had witnessed the positive effects these readings had on people and the transformations they inspired. So Bret and I were simply going to have to find another solution to these problems, aside from quitting.

I was soon to learn that this was just the beginning of the obstacles we would have to overcome in relation to my new work. Before I even knew if the man from the health food store was really going to stay away, I had a woman calling me to inform me that my gift was evil. She was convinced that my ability to see and hear spirits was from the Devil, himself. A religious fanatic of sorts, she quoted the Bible to back up her claims. She wanted me to stop what I was doing, and she made threats as added motivation. While her threats were ambiguous, her tone was definite—stop what I was doing or else!

SKEPTICISM AND RELATIVES

I eventually accepted these nerve-racking incidents as side effects to doing this work. But the trials didn't end with strangers; relatives had their own issues with my work. As news about my readings spread, so did the fear of how it would affect the reputation of certain relatives. My own husband was among this group.

Bret is a business owner with strong ties in the community. His father, my father-in-law, owns the business with Bret and was active in the town Rotary Club. So Bret was concerned what people would think if they found out his wife claimed to communicate with spirits. Honestly, I didn't blame him for his concerns. But I couldn't let his fears prevent me from doing this work. And he knew he didn't have the right to ask me to give it up, so he never crossed that line.

Bret never worried that people he knew would learn about my work when I first started out. He figured that nobody was likely to find out if I was only doing a couple readings here and there. Even after Bob and I got interviewed about spirit communication on some major Boston radio stations, Bret figured nobody from Maine was going to hear them. But when I later landed a radio spot every Thursday morning on an FM radio station in Portland, Maine, things were getting a little close to home.

One day Bret picked up a prescription at the pharmacy for me because I had a stomach virus. The pharmacist looked at the bottle and asked, "Vicki Monroe! Is this the Vicki Monroe on the radio?" Bret denied it, telling him the woman on the radio was somebody else. He still didn't want to be associated with that controversial part of me and he was pleased that being on the radio maintained both my anonymity and his.

Then I got a four-show series on television—on the local UPN/WB network—to demonstrate spirit communication with a live audience. The TV station promoted it pretty heavily with a commercial that showed my face to just about every resident of Maine. That was the end of anonymity as I knew it. After the commercials, alone, I couldn't go grocery shopping without someone asking who I saw (in spirit) around them. Then, after the actual shows aired, shopping in Maine was nearly impossible. And since most everyone who knew Bret knew what his wife looked like, that was the end of his anonymity, too.

I know a psychic medium who changed his name before going public with his gift, which is a pretty good idea when it comes to family. His reasoning behind it was that he didn't want to expose his family members to the stigma associated with his work. My problem with doing that is that I would worry how that would appear if people found out about it. Would it appear that I was lying to the public? Would people question the legitimacy of my gift if they found out I wasn't being honest about my name? I never thought of the idea until it was too late anyway, but I don't think I would have changed my name even if I *had* thought of it. Bret, on the other hand, would have loved the idea.

Bret eventually became used to the publicity I was getting and finally succumbed to the fact that his wife was a spirit messenger. I'd say he grew into it slowly. He learned that not only did people *not* judge him for his wife's bizarre abilities, but also, many were actually interested in what I did for a living. And as my readings increasingly booked as much as one to two years into the future, I think Bret was actually proud of me when people he knew called him for favors trying to get an appointment without waiting two years. With time, Bret's fears of what other people felt disappeared altogether. Today, he is not only proud of me, he does everything he can to support my career and my mission to spread my message.

This was true for many of my relatives. At first some were fearful about how my public exposure would affect them. One relative even called me after being interviewed by Bob with some pretty nasty things to say to me. As soon as I answered the phone, I heard, "What the fu#k is this, Vicki? Are you telling *everyone's* life story? Just because you don't care what other people think about you doesn't mean everyone else wants to be dragged down with you!"

Nonetheless, that was three years ago. Today this same person is happy admitting they are related to me, but Bob has still agreed not to write about the interview just to be safe.

SKEPTICISM AND FRIENDS

Friends aren't immune from the implications of knowing me, either. One friend, who often helps me at my live events, can't get her husband to come near me. He won't even come into the hotel lobby on the night of my events when he drops her off. Bret and I used to go out to dinner with them before I "came out" as a spirit messenger, but now I'm someone he'd prefer to avoid. While I'm getting used to this reaction from people, I feel bad that my friend gets caught in the middle. It also saddens me that we will never go out as couples again. But I understand that he *doesn't* understand, and this creates fear that is easier for him to avoid than it is to face.

Other friends have also had to deal with the public disdain of hanging around with a spirit messenger. Once, upon entering a restaurant for dinner, a group of women finishing their meals starting squabbling when they saw me, rather loudly I must add. One woman, in particular, made a scene.

"Oh my God. That's her, isn't it? Don't let her look at me. Is she looking at me? Waitress, where's our bill? We have to get out of here. We can't be in this restaurant if she's here."

It was quite a spectacle, and uncomfortable for everyone. Needless to say, I wasn't asked to sign any autographs. Once my friends got over the surprise of it, they laughed about it. Still, I think my friends walk around with me with a little apprehension of a repeat performance from someone. Who can blame them? I'm apprehensive every so often, myself.

This is a sampling of the challenges influenced by skepticism that I have had to deal with as a spirit messenger. A lot of people comment to me that it must be great to have this gift. It is. I couldn't imagine a more fulfilling career. Still, it has its drawbacks. But what makes these drawbacks easier to take is witnessing the comfort, peace of mind, renewed faith and joy that messages from spirit provide people. These benefits far outweigh any skepticism that crosses my path.

PART III
Understanding "Knowing"

CHAPTER SEVEN
BELIEVING & KNOWING

By Bob Olson

*There is a limit where the intellect fails and breaks down,
and this limit is where the questions concerning God, and
freewill, and immortality arise.*

~ *Kant*

It wasn't until October of 1999 that I finally recognized there is a difference between "believing" and "knowing." By this time, ten months after first meeting Vicki, I felt I had read every book worth reading on the subject of psychic mediums. I was no longer discovering new enlightening insights with every book. In fact, I was growing somewhat bored with the research because it was all so repetitive; which, to me, was a statement of validity in itself because the mediums were teaching many of the same principles. But I knew I needed a method for obtaining alternative perspectives for my book, so it occurred to me that it was time to conduct some more interviews.

I immediately set out to interview about thirty of Vicki's clients, friends and relatives. While conducting these interviews, I repeatedly asked a few template questions at the end of each conversation. One of the questions I asked involved the issue of stigma. My question to each person was, "Have you felt the stigma associated with being a 'believer' while telling people about Vicki and her gift?"

The answers I received from almost every interviewee were similar; everyone was aware of the stigma but nobody worried about it. Unexpectedly, during one of the last interviews I conducted, I came to the stunning realization that my use of the word "believer" was in poor choice. And I owe this recognition to one very perceptive woman whom I interviewed.

OBJECTING TO THE WORD "BELIEVER"

Her name is M. E. Oriol, an author who specializes in life-coaching, pastoral counseling and psychotherapy. Oh, how envious I am of her name, M. E. Oriol, flaunting the intonation of a distinguished writer—as opposed to Bob Olson, which flaunts the intonation of common and ordinary.

Ms. Oriol is a person who takes pride in her command of the English language. Not surprisingly, she also teaches English as a second language to adult students, mostly professionals from other countries who want to learn English, but also to students from this country who do not speak, read or write the language. Perhaps Ms. Oriol's cautious way with words is a hazard of this profession, but I sense it is more a desire to accurately express what she wishes to communicate. And since finding the correct word or phrase is so gratifying to me as a writer—like striking the correct note on a piano, or perfectly connecting a baseball bat to a ball—I was pleasantly immersed in my conversation with Ms. Oriol. It was refreshing that she not only carefully selected her own words, she also politely reprimanded *me* when I asked a question that was vaguely worded or presumptive in its context.

When I began to ask Ms. Oriol the question about the stigma of being a believer, my mind leaped ahead with a clear premonition of her response; our conversation had trained me to know she would find fault with my use of the word "believer." As my mind quickly imagined the debate, I predicted her objection to the word.

Stumbling to a silence in mid-sentence, I said, "This is interesting. I have asked the same question to almost thirty people, but now I realize I have worded it incorrectly. I was about to ask if you have felt the stigma associated with being a believer. But now I know that the word 'believer' is a misleading and assumptive choice. It is misleading because believing is not the state of mind that I wish to express. And it is assumptive because it automatically assumes that what is 'believed' might *not* be true. I guess the word I should be using is 'knower.' So my question to you is, have you ever felt the stigma associated with being a *knower*?"

REDEFINING MYSELF A "KNOWER"

From that conversation I had redefined myself a knower. Believers are people who accept, on faith, the dogma of others and assume it to be true. Knowers are people who have firsthand knowledge to support their convictions, personal evidence that allows them to *know* it is true. However, that evidence need not come from a third party such as a spirit messenger. For many, they are open and aware enough to see the evidence on their own, the multitude of signs and messages that surround us every day. I was not one of those people.

Ms. Oriol happens to be one of those people who enjoys a knowing founded on personal awareness. At the age of twenty, more than three decades ago, she decided to look outside her parents' religion to discover a relationship with God that was better aligned with her own truth. "I decided it was between me and God," she explained. "At this point, I read everything I could get my hands on related to spiritualism, God, psychology and philosophy. I was evolving into my own self and my own relationship with God." In her exploration, Ms. Oriol discovered " a religion that seemed to be a greater—not final—but a greater truth" for her. Hence, she converted. Years later, she became a minister with this religion.

The most obvious, and attractive, expression of Ms. Oriol's knowing is her sense of freedom—freedom from her attachment to the beliefs and opinions of others. When asked if she was skeptical the first time she heard of Vicki's gift, she replied, "No, not at all, because I am neutral in it. If somebody shares that with me, I have no judgment on it. Later, if I witness it, it becomes and that is fun. I didn't think she was a fraud right off the start *because* I am neutral. Why would I doubt it? I haven't lost anything if she can't do what she says she can do. There is freedom in being neutral."

Needless to say, Ms. Oriol is unaffected by the stigma associate with being a knower. Still, for unrelated reasons, she considers her spiritual way of life a private matter. For years she rarely talked about it. "It was just too sacred," she admitted. "I do not know how to put my experience with it into words. I'll mention it, and if it touches someone's heart and they ask me more, I'll talk to them about it. But I don't want to betray my experience by not portraying it accurately," she said, once again exemplifying her devotion to lexical accuracy.

Beyond any doubt, Ms. Oriol is a knower. She described her relationship with God as a "personal experience." Not once did she refer to a book or a lesson taught by someone else as her basis or foundation for knowing. They may have paved the road for her, but she walked it. For her, knowing came from something she experienced from within. Although she never revealed to me what those experiences were—probably because they were too sacred and profound to describe—one only needs to be in her presence to sense her knowing energy.

The lesson I learned from Ms. Oriol is that there is a difference between believing and knowing. It took me ten months of research and readings, and thirty interviews to discover this lesson. My initial three-hour reading with Vicki did *not* instantly convert me from skeptic to knower; I first had to pass through the believer stage. Due to years of skepticism, my intellect fought the paradigm shift. Nevertheless, after months of continuous reinforcing effort, I finally grew into and owned my new knower status. I still have far to go and admit that I am no spiritual authority, but the rewards of knowing are far greater than I would ever have predicted.

CHAPTER EIGHT
KNOWING IS A PROCESS AND NOT AN EVENT

By Bob Olson

Faith and doubt go hand in hand, they are complementaries.
One who never doubts will never truly believe.

~ Hermann Hesse

For my birthday, my wife, Melissa, gave me a blue baseball cap that had red and white letters on it that spelled "Red Sox." It was in memory of my father because he loved the Red Sox; and, according to Vicki, he is now an even more devoted fan in the spirit world. Considering the unexpected reunion with my father just months prior (at my first reading), this baseball cap was the most meaningful birthday gift I received that year.

DEEPENING MY FAITH: THE BASEBALL CAP STORY

A couple weeks after my birthday, Vicki sent me an email expressing some guidance from my father. It was not uncommon that he would visit her when he had a message for me. At the end of her email she wrote, "Did your father used to wear a hat?" The question just hung there without any explanation, so it appeared nonsensical. I was certain that

Vicki was confused, as my father was not one to wear a hat. So I dismissed the question without a response.

Two weeks later, Melissa and I traveled to Maine and had dinner with Vicki and her mother, Nancy. Since Vicki's accuracy had been uncanny throughout our, now, five months of telephone conversations and email correspondence, the hat snafu was still bugging me. So I challenged her on it.

"Okay Vicki, what's all this talk about my father wearing a hat? Because, except for a cowboy hat that he occasionally wore while driving a truck, he wasn't one to wear hats," I contested.

Vicki went into her semi-trance mode right there at the restaurant table, that state of mind where she's obviously tuning in to some beacon of information which is indiscernible to the rest of us. "Oh, oh..." she begins, with a halting speech pattern that indicates to me that some message is coming through. "Your father keeps showing me this hat he's wearing. He keeps taking it off and placing it back on his head. He was doing this while I was writing that email to you last month. It's a blue baseball cap with red and white lettering that spells 'Red Sox' across the front."

Melissa and I just sat in dead-silence for about twenty seconds. I recall cocking my head to the side while looking at Vicki, like a dog might do when you play a harmonica or whistle a tune. Vicki and Nancy just smirked at one another knowing Vicki had, once again, struck an impressionable chord.

I hated to admit it, but I needed these "baseball cap" moments to further deepen my faith. I wanted to buy into the conclusion that my initial three-hour reading in January was enough to convert me from stone-blind skeptic to unshakable knower; but, in retrospect, I discovered that *becoming a knower is a process, not an event.*

My first reading with Vicki catapulted me to a new level of enlightenment, but even at this level I was still a freshman who needed to grow accustomed to my new paradigm shift. The truth was that I needed to ripen spiritually before I was ready to begin writing this book. At the time of this baseball cap moment, it would be another year-and-a-half before I would put my fingers to the keyboard. So much for my lightning bolt enlightenment. I guess I'm a slow learner.

Accordingly, my process required *many* "baseball cap" moments. My intellect continuously fought what I knew to be true. With the passing of days, weeks and months after an incredible reading, my intellect slowly brainwashed me into questioning what I once thought would be undeniable experiences. But denial is a powerful force. The result of this inner-conflict was that my beliefs were very shakable, and periodically needed reinforcement in the form of *additional* evidence. If it were not for Vicki's assistance, I suspect my spiritual growth may never have traveled fast enough to fly, but rather, would have crashed and burned on the runway.

DEEPENING MY FAITH: THE SCRAPPER STORY

Being blessed with such a gifted friend, I often made use of Vicki's talents when my newly found belief-system grew frail. One day, while I interviewed Vicki by phone, I was engrossed by an eerie scene before me. I was walking through my living room because I'm a pacer—I pace while I talk on the phone. As I looked out my sliding glass door, the neighbor's cat, Scrapper, was walking up our brick walkway toward the living room where I paced.

Now, Scrapper is a beastly creature. I think he was

squashed by an eighteen-wheeler and came back to life—he's not a pretty sight. And he's got a temper to suit his appearance. Once, when I lowered my defenses to try patting him, he taught me that if a cat looks like a rabid beast, I should take that as a warning. Since this momentary lapse of reason resulted in scars that lasted for months, it was a lesson I only needed to learn once.

Scrapper has always respected *my* space as much as I respect his, and he has never come up on our porch. He'll sit on the brick walk and meow for my own cat, Pesky, to come out and play. But he does this at a safe distance. This particular day, however, I just knew Scrapper was heading for the porch. I sensed it in his stride. And he did. He came strolling down the walk and right onto our porch directly in front of the sliding glass door. As he stood there, staring me square in the eye, he meowed. I couldn't hear him because the door was closed, but I could see his mouth moving. It was so unusual and out-of-character for Scrapper to do this that it was spine-chilling. Looking into his vacant black eyes, I got the creeps so bad I had to leave the room and retreat to my office.

Once seated at my desk, and trying to forget about this bizarre Scrapper incident, I continued interviewing Vicki. After gathering the nerve to test her once again, I asked Vicki which spirit-guide was presently watching over me. I always felt guilty testing her, but I needed a boost this particular day as my faith was fading from having a troublesome week. She informed me, without delay, that "Etheria" was by my side helping me write this book. Etheria is a penetrating soul who is Vicki's principal spirit-guide. Prying, I asked, "How do I *really* know Etheria is with me right now?"—feeling somewhat ashamed of my doubtful challenge.

After a short hesitation, as if someone in the room was

talking to her, Vicki nonchalantly replied, "Is there a cat meowing at your door right now? This isn't your cat, but another cat?"

I was awestricken. I looked out my office window to see if Scrapper was still there, and he was, still meowing at the door. All I could say to Vicki was, "Okay, that's enough proof for me." I had my evidence fix and was good-to-go for another few months.

KNOWING IS A PROCESS AND NOT AN EVENT

Without exception, I found I needed an additional layer of evidence to reinforce my beliefs every couple months during the first ten months of my journey. It was these "baseball cap" and "Scrapper" type episodes that sustained my process for spiritual growth, empowering my faith and reaffirming the miracles I had slowly begun to question over time. Time seemed to have a way of diminishing my convictions, making me question myself and my memories of all the prior evidence. Similar to the way time diminishes the pain of a loved-one's death, after a while it feels less like reality and more like a dream. Vicki, along with the spirit-guides who worked with us, always remained patient with my periodic testing of Vicki's abilities. In the end, I don't know precisely when it occurred, we eventually pierced my final layer of skeptical skin.

I'm not sure exactly how much evidence was required to end my inner-conflict between faith and intellect. All I know is that about ten months into my research and investigation of psychic mediums, my belief became a "knowing." The change was subtle and slow, but I now realize this is a life-long change that I *own*. Further, this knowing runs deeper with every new day. It's like learning to walk or drive. One day you realize you are doing it without thinking about it. I guess it's the difference between memorizing information and absorbing it subconsciously through experience. Once the foundation of knowledge is laid, experience is always the better teacher.

CHAPTER NINE
KNOWING THE APPROPRIATE USE OF MY GIFT

By Vicki Monroe

Never be ashamed to own you have been in the wrong; 'tis but saying you are wiser today than you were yesterday.

~ *Jonathan Swift*

In the chapters preceding this one, Bob wrote about the subject of "knowing." In its most basic sense, he is referring to the stage beyond belief, where one acquires an inner knowing that we do not die, that there is an afterlife and that spirit communication is possible. This type of knowing is a level of spiritual growth that produces benefits such as peace of mind, patience and even empowerment.

In this chapter, I want to share with you a different kind of knowing that I had to learn, that is, knowing how and when to properly use my ability of spirit communication. Through trial and error, I acquired a knowing of what boundaries to draw with spirits, as well as when and where to pass along their messages. I think some of these stories may surprise you, might possibly shock you, or will, at least, get you thinking about the responsibilities and implications of being a spirit messenger. Since psychic mediums aren't given a training manual with their abilities, we must learn how to use them properly through trial and error unless we are lucky enough to find a teacher or mentor early on. I wasn't that lucky.

Shortly after I began doing readings professionally, my husband, Bret, and I went to Florida. It was a business trip for Bret but a vacation for me. For the first time in my life, I had been doing a lot of readings and seriously needed some downtime to rejuvenate.

LEARNING MY BOUNDARIES AMONG STRANGERS

With all the positive publicity and new clients I was attracting, I had finally overcome my childhood fears of not being accepted due to my abilities. For the first time in my life, it felt good to be a spirit messenger. I felt purpose. I was helping people. And, at last, I was able to let my guard down and be comfortable with who I am.

After we arrived in Florida, Bret and I went to get a bite to eat at a restaurant in the hotel where we were staying. When the waiter came to our table, I immediately saw what I believed must be his grandmother in spirit. She began giving me messages as he asked about our order. I tried ignoring her, but she wouldn't stop. It was like trying to have a conversation while someone keeps interrupting, a situation in which every mother of young children is familiar.

I was looking at the menu and noticed they offered peanut butter sandwiches, one of Bret's favorites. I looked up at Bret and said, "Hey, did you notice they have peanut butter sandwiches?" At the same moment, the grandmother figure told me that our waiter was allergic to peanut butter. Without thinking, I looked up at the waiter and said, "Oh, you're allergic to peanut butter. Then we won't order that."

The waiter froze. "How did you know that?" he asked.

The look on his face made me realize he wasn't impressed; rather, he looked frightened. Not knowing how to answer his question without freaking him out more, I just shrugged my shoulders and said, "Lucky guess?"

The waiter took our order but never came back. Someone else brought us our order and bill. In fact, he must have stayed clear of me during our entire stay because I never saw him again, and we ate at that restaurant a lot! While this might have all been a coincidence (I'd like to think), it was one of my early lessons as an adult on choosing when to give messages and when to keep my mouth shut.

Obviously, it wasn't me that I was concerned about; it was the waiter. There were people from several different cultures working at that hotel, and I'm sure some cultures would associate my gift with evil. In Maine, I didn't really run into this issue. Most Mainers might just think I'm a fruitcake, but that's different than making a waiter think that Satan is ordering a peanut butter sandwich from him. So even though it was never my intention to reveal my ability to the waiter, the experience taught me to be extra careful in certain situations.

LEARNING MY BOUNDARIES AMONG BUSINESS ASSOCIATES

The next evening, Bret and I had dinner with a married couple who worked for Bret's company. Bret left the table to do something with the husband, Pat, while leaving me alone at the table with Pat's wife, Alie. During our conversation, I began seeing Alie's spirits. These spirits really wanted me to give Alie some messages, and since the spirits claimed that these messages were very important to Alie, I found myself in a dilemma. After careful consideration, I did what I felt compelled to do—I relayed the messages. Fortunately, Alie was both open to the information and appreciative of it.

Bret later learned that I gave Alie a brief reading at the restaurant. Since Alie hadn't known anything about my abilities prior to this dinner, Bret thought it was inappropriate for me to initiate the reading during a business engagement. "Who knows how any one person will respond?" Bret reasoned. "It could have had a negative effect on the business relationship, and it probably wasn't worth the risk," he added.

Naturally, Bret's feelings brought me back to the time when he didn't want anyone to know what I did for fear of what others would think. But Bret didn't feel that fear anymore and this situation was different. This was Bret's work, his employees, and he was right—it probably wasn't worth the risk. It wasn't as if Alie's spirits couldn't have got those messages to her in other ways. I was simply the easiest way to deliver them, the most direct route. But there are millions of people in this world who don't have a psychic medium— don't even believe in psychic mediums—to pass along such messages for them. This doesn't mean these people won't get these messages. They probably will, just in other ways, such as in dreams, through meditation or through their own intuition, to name just a few.

It was difficult to accept that I still need to be selective with whom I shared my ability, but I realized that I never know how anyone will respond to it. For this reason, it makes more sense to put myself out there in the public eye so that people who are interested can come to me, rather than me trying to find them. The truth is that whenever I walk into a store or restaurant, I see spirits around just about everyone. These spirits all know I'm there and they all want me to help them get their messages across. But not everyone is ready to hear from their spirits. Even if the messages were delivered, many people would ignore them. People need to be ready. I'm sure everyone could benefit from a massage, too; but massage therapists don't walk up to strangers in the street and start squeezing their shoulders.

What types of messages do most spirits want to convey? They run the gamut, but most spirits just want their loved-ones to know that they are okay, that they have not "died" but have merely crossed over to the other side, that they are closer to them than they ever were, and that they will be there to greet them when it is their time to return home. Sometimes there are messages of forgiveness or requests to be forgiven. And every so often there are messages to encourage people to follow what their instincts are already telling them: go back to school, take the job you really want regardless of the smaller salary, ditch that creep who is abusing you, start treating your body better (eating right, stop smoking, reduce stress), and similar messages that are more confirming of what you already know, rather than telling you something new.

While these messages can be life transforming, they are not a matter of life and death. I have never given someone a message that literally saved their life, mainly because I have never given a message that someone could not obtain in other ways without a psychic medium, such as through their intuition, meditation, automatic writing or prayer. My ability is only a tool like a telephone is a tool, a link from the spirit world to you. While there are life-changing benefits to receiving messages from spirit, these benefits only manifest if and when the person receiving them is disposed to making use of them. This I now know. Yet, this was a knowing that I needed to acquire. And my experiences with the waiter and

Alie, as well as those I'm about to share with you, helped me to acquire this knowing.

LEARNING TO GIVE MESSAGES WHILE PROTECTING MY BOUNDARIES

While still in Florida, I was having a bite to eat (yes, again) with Bret at the hotel restaurant. As was normal for this trip, I was seeing spirits everywhere hovering around most every restaurant patron and employee. Some people had one spirit with them. Some people had two or three or even six. I was learning how to signal to these spirits that I was "off duty." Surely, I couldn't be giving readings to everybody, especially after the incident with the waiter. So I sent out a signal using my thoughts asking the spirits to respect my privacy.

Imagine, however, that you are a spirit and you have something that is important to you that you wish to convey to someone in our world. Suddenly, in walks a spirit messenger like myself. What would you do? The spirit messenger is clearly sending out a signal to be left alone, but you are the persistent type and really want to get your message across. You can do it in other ways, of course, but that usually requires more time and effort. So, being an impatient spirit—since we do retain much of our personality on the other side—what are you likely to do?

Well, one such spirit was in the restaurant that day. It was a grandmother figure whom I first saw while I was eating, but didn't think much about until she followed me towards the elevator as I was leaving the restaurant. Bret left for a meeting and I was going to our hotel room to get ready for some fun in the Florida sun.

I hoped the grandmother would get the message that I needed to relax, but when she followed me into the elevator,

I knew she didn't care much about my R-and-R. She was a feisty one and was pretty upset with the hotel management. She was bothered by the unnecessary amounts of food being wasted. They were just throwing away all the muffins, pastries and bagels that were not being used each day. And she wanted me to make a formal complaint to the woman at the bakery counter, named Emily.

Now, I knew I shouldn't let a spirit push me around. I remembered watching the movie *The Sixth Sense*, where that cute little boy ran around doing errands for the spirits, and I remembered thinking how he needed to learn to draw the line somewhere or he'd have spirits bullying him to do all sorts of crazy things. Nonetheless, this feisty little grandmother hit a soft spot in me, so I agreed to make the complaint for her, using my name—not hers.

I found Emily at the bakery counter and told her I wanted to make a formal complaint. She actually gave me some papers to fill out, which I completed. When I told her what the complaint was for, it was like one of those light bulbs went off in her head. She said that the wasted food had been bothering her for a long time, but she was too afraid to try doing something about it. She knew there were plenty of shelters in the area that would be happy to take the food. After all, it wasn't spoiled or stale, it was just one day old. She said she was relieved to now have a complaint she could take to management.

Suddenly, I realized that the grandmother in the elevator belonged to Emily. Emily's grandmother knew this was bothering Emily and wanted to help her find a solution. I was moved by this grandmother's efforts to help her granddaughter. It was a perfect example of how spirits help to guide and assist us in life.

What did I learn from this experience? Well, first I learned that I needed to be more assertive with spirits and not let them push me around. That's a lesson that took a long time. Second, I learned that there are ways to use my gift without freaking anyone out. In this case, I didn't tell Emily that I was a spirit messenger and that a spirit asked me to make the complaint. That might have given Emily a heart attack or got me thrown out of the hotel. Instead, I just made the complaint for the grandmother and left it at that. It felt good to me. It made the grandmother happy. It gave Emily a reason to do something about an issue that had been bothering her. And, who knows, it might have set things in motion to do something good with the food, as well.

LEARNING MY BOUNDARIES ON MATTERS THAT DON'T INVOLVE ME

Upon returning home from Florida, I was looking over the prior week's newspapers to see what local news I had missed. One story reported the murder of a teenage girl in a nearby town. While reading the article, I looked up from my newspaper to see the girl standing in front of me—in spirit, that is. The girl then proceeded to give me much more detailed information about the crime than the article had revealed.

Although the murderer was still unknown by police, the little girl told me it was her father who killed her. "It was an accident," she said. "He was upset with me. We got into an argument and he killed me in his rage."

She went on to explain that her father then left her body in a place where it would be found. He didn't just dump the body. He carefully laid her beside the road, leaving her clothing and hair meticulously in place. He didn't want his pretty little girl looking unsightly.

The first thing that went through my mind was, "What am I supposed to do with this information?" Apparently, she heard my thoughts and told me that there was nothing I could do. She said that her mother would not be able to accept that her husband killed their child. She also added that he would die of a heart attack in about a year, which later came true.

This was a situation where the spirit taught me what to do before I learned the hard way, for instance, by trying to tell the police what this spirit had told me. This young girl was the first crime victim to appear before me outside of a reading, but she would not be the last. What I have realized is that these spirits never come to me to solve their crimes. While I have often received calls from family members of these victims for readings—probably because most of these cases were local—that hasn't always been the case. Sometimes I have simply watched a television talk show where guests were discussing stories of their missing loved-ones and, instantly, the missing person would appear in front of me; that is, if they had passed.

I can't tell you for sure why these spirits visit me, especially since most do not ask me to get involved in their pending criminal investigations. Sure, I would love to help the police if they asked me for assistance. But they don't. They know who I am and what I do, but they don't call asking for my help. And who can blame them? The district attorney's office needs evidence that can be used in court, and clues delivered from spirit messengers do not fall under the heading of "credible evidence." So, don't worry criminals; I'm no threat to you. If I tried to tell people about my spirit communications, I would probably get locked up faster than you.

I presume that these spirits visit me simply because they can and possibly because it is comforting to them, like sharing a secret with someone. You know how some secrets just burn away at you until you share them with someone? Perhaps that is the reason spirit-victims of crime come knocking on my ethereal door. Maybe they merely need to share. While I wish I had the answer to all these spiritual riddles, I don't. I believe that we sometimes just need to accept what is without always knowing why.

KNOWING MY BOUNDARIES AND GETTING IT RIGHT

Many months after learning the lessons surrounding the Florida trip, I again met the victim of another murder. At first, I saw the young woman in spirit while she was still considered missing. As a mother, myself, I wanted to help the mother of this young lady, but I now knew there was a proper order to all this. Sure enough, the mother soon called for a reading.

Now I was presented with a new lesson: how to gently inform someone that their loved-one has passed while they are clinging to hope that they are still alive. This mother made it easy for me because she listened to her intuition.

"Am I right?" she asked.

"Yes, you are right," I said.

"I needed to know," she said, "because now I can move on and find out who did it. Plus I needed to know she wasn't suffering somewhere," she said with a tearful burst of relief and grief.

As I proceeded with the reading, I provided detailed evidence about the crime scene—evidence not released to the public—to prove to the mother that her daughter was, in fact, providing me with this information. She even gave me the first names of the people connected with her murder. Both names were familiar to the mother, and one of these people was later arrested after valuable evidence was found to incriminate him. The arrest did not in any way result from her reading with me. It was merely confirmation for the mother that everything I told her was true.

The "knowing" I have gained with experience from hundreds of readings each year has taught me that my ability to communicate with spirits doesn't exist to solve crimes. While this might not be the path of other mediums, this is my truth. I believe my abilities may help in some investigations, but it is more needed in helping those left behind, in this world, to work through their grief so that they are better able to move forward and enjoy life in the face of their loss. And this is a process that need not be rushed. Every individual must handle this challenge in their own way, on their own schedule.

PRACTICE MAKES PERFECT

Psychic mediums often acquire a knowing about life-after-death that results from their ability to see, hear or communicate with spirits. This is a subtle process that deepens with time and experience and seems quite natural. What is less innate is the ability to know how and when to properly use this "gift." I learned by trial and error.

The examples I mentioned above are just a few of the many experiences that helped shape, guide and train me to use my abilities properly. As I said, we aren't born with a training manual. So, like with any ability, practice makes perfect. Well, that cliché is a bit of a misnomer considering the truth of another cliché, "nobody's perfect." I have to admit I still like to shake up a waiter now and then, especially the macho type who patronizes women.

PART IV
Separate Journeys

CHAPTER TEN
A MEDIUM'S JOURNEY OF EMPOWERMENT

By Vicki Monroe

What do you have to fear? Nothing. Whom do you have to fear? No one. Why? Because whoever has joined forces with God obtains three great privileges: omnipotence without power, intoxication without wine, and life without death.

~ St. Francis of Assisi

About eight months after Bob's first reading, he and Melissa completed a book tour for Bob's first book, *Win The Battle*. Melissa was a big part of that book, so they did all the publicity together. As they told me about the TV, radio and magazine interviews they were doing, it prepared me for what was to come.

Since Bob and Melissa did more book publicity on radio than in any other media, they made a lot of valuable connections with radio hosts and producers and became well-practiced at speaking on the radio. As a result, one radio host with whom they became friends, John Alexandrov, asked them to fill in for him one day while he was on vacation. The show they presented was such a success with John's audience that he asked them to fill in for him again a couple months later.

This time, Bob and Melissa asked John if they could invite me on the show as their guest. John and the station managers were open to the idea of having a psychic on the air, although I don't think they understood what the term "psychic medium" meant. Nevertheless, Bob and Melissa asked me if I'd do it.

STAGE FRIGHT

I had never considered appearing on a radio show. Even if I had, I would have been too fearful to give it a second thought. So when Bob and Melissa called to invite me to do the show with them, I didn't know whether to run or hide. So I said, "Yes, I'll do it!" Then, after hanging up the phone, I immediately panicked!

For two months before the show, my heart pounded in fright at the very thought of being heard by thousands of people at one time. Some people say I'm a natural for radio, but there is nothing natural about it—I was scared from the get-go.

Bob and Melissa comforted my anxieties about doing the show and gave me confidence that it was the right thing to do. "Hey," Bob teased, "even if you choke and burn, you can touch thousands of lives in a single two-hour show with the same message you give people in your private readings—one person at a time."

In spite of Bob's cute little "choke and burn" comment that he so subtly threw into his encouragement, I liked what he said. I realized that sometimes we have to take risks in order to grow. My only risk was personal embarrassment. The upside was that masses of people might discover something they didn't think was possible—spirit communication. So we planned the show which would air live on the same night the movie *The Sixth Sense* was to open. The timing was perfect.

IT'S SHOWTIME... HELP!

By the night of the show, I hadn't slept in days. I had no idea of what to expect. I wasn't even sure if I my abilities would work on the radio! Would I be able to give a reading by phone? All my client readings thus far were in person. Bob was sure I could do it because I had given him readings numerous times over the phone. I just didn't see those as normal readings since Bob wasn't really a client anymore; we were just two friends chatting. So for two months I fearfully imagined humiliating myself on live radio. Now the moment had arrived.

The show ran from five to seven o'clock on a Friday night. We arrived at the station like a rock band—Bob, Melissa, my husband, Bret, my mother, Nancy, and me. We were early, but the tiny studio was empty so we piled in. Melissa introduced me to the controls, the headphones and the microphones. We picked out where we would all sit—first Bob, Melissa to his right and me to her right—so Bob could ask the questions and see both of us at the same time. Once Bob got his outline in front of him, we were ready to roll.

Clyde, the control operator, arrived and carefully instructed Bob on what to say before and after each commercial: the station call letters, the telephone numbers and the time. Clyde handled all the commercials and music before and after the breaks, as well as the phone lines. Clyde is such a calm, kind soul that he made the two-hour show easy for all of us. When the moment arrived, I was more petrified than ever. Clyde held up his hand as the introductory music began playing. He slowly closed one finger, two, three, four and then five; he then pointed to Bob to begin. I wanted to get up and run out of the studio, but I was stuck in a corner with no place to go.

Melissa and Bob spent the first half-hour telling the story of how we all met and interviewing me about my abilities. John Alexandrov told Bob that the key to a successful radio interview is to get the guest to tell stories. Bob made the mistake of asking me questions that could be answered with a yes or no; and in my fright, that's how I answered them—like a shy child talking to a stranger.

"Is it true that you can actually see and hear spirits, Vicki?" Bob asked me.

"Yes," I answered. Then there was dead silence. I think Bob expected me to elaborate, but my hands were shaking and my mind was blank.

"Could you elaborate on that a little?" Bob said with a big smile on his face. Bob has a good sense of humor and he thought it was funny seeing me so nervous.

"Sure, well, I usually see and hear the spirits, but sometimes I just hear them," I said. That was it. Again, my mind went blank and more dead silence followed.

After a few more questions that went nowhere, it took everything Bob had not to roll in the isles laughing, especially when—in my panicked paralysis—I twice answered by only nodding my head. I would have liked to start laughing, too; but being new to radio, I thought we needed to be serious. So Bob finally started answering the questions himself and asking me to confirm his answers with a yes or no—which, in my defense, I was really good at.

"Is it true that spirits don't like to be considered as dead, but prefer the term 'crossed-over?'" Bob asked.

"Yes, that's true," I answered.

"And the reason for this is that one of the key messages

they want to convey is that they are still alive, still with us, only they are with us in spirit rather than physical form. Is that right?" he said.

"That's correct, they often say they are closer to us now than they ever were," I answered.

This system where Bob gave the question and answer, and then I confirmed the answer as correct wasn't really too bad. At least it was easier. And as I loosened up, I soon started to get my thoughts back and began answering the questions with more detail. However, just as I was beginning to relax, it was time to take callers.

GIVING READINGS OVER THE AIRWAVES

People were supposed to call the station and I would give them a three-to-five-minute reading on the air. Before the first commercial, Bob gave out the studio's telephone number. This was the first time he gave out the number because we didn't want people calling until the interview was over. When Bob asked Clyde during the break if we had any callers yet, Clyde laughed. "Bob, all the phone lines have been jammed since ten-minutes after you started the show. I've never seen anything like it," he said. That was reassuring to me. My first concern was that nobody would call. Now that I didn't have to worry about that anymore, I could feel my eyes becoming glossy with nervousness that it was now time to perform.

Bob has this theory about doing something in front of an audience for the first time: if you are excited and prepared, there is something magical about the newness of the experience that gets captured in your enthusiasm. Even if you are scared silly, this edge-of-your-seat enthusiasm will result in one of your best performances—not necessarily the smoothest, but one you will forever recall with a smile. I prayed that he was right, and that's exactly what happened this particular Friday evening. I could see Clyde's face as I did each reading. Every time I nailed a detail like, "You have two daughters who are deaf?" and the caller replied affirmatively, Clyde would look at Bob and Melissa and mouth the words, "Oh my God!" He had a smile planted on his face the whole night, and his reactions helped boost my confidence that I was doing okay.

Despite my tenseness, I plowed through my fears and showed twenty thousand listeners what a reading from a psychic medium can be like. I knew people were used to hearing psychics on the radio who give advice about relationships or career issues; but at this time in history, which was about a year before John Edward's TV show began, few people understood that it was possible to communicate with spirits. My goal that night was to deliver accurately detailed messages about caller's lives that I could never have known if not for a relative from the spirit world whispering them into my ear. And while it wasn't my best radio performance ever, the spirits provided me with stunning evidence that got people questioning their beliefs.

As expected, there were a few skeptics who called. At first I was scared, not knowing what to expect. Their voices were tense, serious and distrustful. But the spirits who came through made me realize that these people called for a reason. They wanted to believe and they wanted me to help them with it. Some were resistant, almost defensive, with the messages I gave them. And who wouldn't be? Hearing me offer evidence that we survive death shakes up a skeptic's world. Some people were relieved, some extremely grateful, and others were quite disturbed that a lifetime of learned beliefs were now in question. So a few people's belief systems got rattled that night, but it gave them something to think about over the next few days and weeks.

WITNESSING THE BENEFITS A READING CAN OFFER

Meanwhile, Bret and my mother watched the show from the hallway through a big window. They could hear everything including the callers' voices from a speaker, which they had cranked up loud. This was the first time Bret had ever really watched me give a reading. He was never really interested in my readings, so it was a breakthrough of sorts, as he finally got to witness the precious value that messages from spirit offer people.

Communicating with a deceased loved-one tends to squeeze out a few tears with most people. It is like a family reunion with someone you never thought you'd hear from again, at least not in this lifetime. This is one of the reasons Bob sobbed like a lost little boy for two-hours during his first reading. It is also why I keep boxes of tissues handy in my office and at my medium demonstrations, so people can sop up their tears during their readings. And, from what my mother tells me, it is also the reason that Bret had to keep stepping from the hallway into the men's room during the radio show. It must have been a surreal experience as he listened to the readings and gained a newfound understanding for the benefits that my "little hobby" offers to the world.

The radio station's caller lines were gridlocked the entire show. The public couldn't get enough; everyone wanted to get a reading. Before we could catch a breath, the two hours were over. All of us were exhausted from the stress of it. We went to dinner to deactivate our stress-levels and talk about the experience. Little did we know, this would be the first of *many* radio shows. It was like the first dip of a roller coaster that is so scary you are ready to call it quits, yet you still have a bunch of twists, turns and somersaults to get through before it's over.

After Bret, my mother and I left Bob and Melissa's house that night just after eleven o'clock, Bob and Melissa went to the midnight showing of *The Sixth Sense*. As I mentioned, it was the first night the movie opened. Bob said, "It was the perfect ending to an evening spent with a gal who 'sees dead people.'" Little did we know, this movie would catapult the public's interest of mediumship into overdrive.

HOOKED ON THE RIPPLE EFFECT

After the show, I was hooked. People began calling and emailing me, sharing how the show brought them peace, comfort and renewed faith. Many of these people called for personal readings, claiming that the show helped them overcome their skepticism enough to give a personal reading a try. This demonstrated to me that our message was heard; and that, by putting myself in the public eye, it really would attract people who were ready to hear messages from their spirits. For the first time, I felt I truly understood how the ripple effect worked, and now I wanted to create more ripples.

The next day, I called Bob and said, "When can we do it again?" I thought he'd laugh at me; but instead, he said he would get in touch with some radio hosts and producers he had met during his book tour. The next day, we were booked on two radio shows in Boston; and within a week, we began doing interviews over the phone on radio shows across the country. Then, within two months, we were doing our own radio show, *The Spirit Communication Hour*, on a national radio network.

For two hours a week over the next several months, we presented *The Spirit Communication Hour with Bob Olson and Vicki Monroe*. Bob played the semi-skeptic host while I gave readings to radio callers. Basically, he knew what the skeptics were thinking when I gave readings, and he confronted me with their questions and concerns.

"Vicki, telling the caller that she's at a crossroads… isn't that a little general and obvious? Heck, everyone I know is at a crossroads in their life," responded Bob to a reading I started with a caller named Joan.

"That's true. But that's what Joan's grandmother showed me—a fork in the road, which means her granddaughter is at a crossroads in her life. Basically, she's leading me to know which direction the reading is going. Now I know we're not talking about her health or her relationships. The grandmother would have given me different symbols for that. Now I know that we are going to be talking about a job change, school or something of that nature," I told Bob.

Bob and I worked great together, playing off one another like an old married couple. Bob would ask me to explain what I was seeing and hearing, and would question me when a message sounded too vague to be believable. It helped the skeptics listening to the show, because Bob would ask the questions that were running through their mind. And it helped train me to understand how skeptics think so that I could give better evidence during a reading.

SEPARATE JOURNEYS

The show was a success in audience participation and we quickly gained an established following, but the "national audience" wasn't as large as the network's representative made it sound. Since our contract was ending, we had to decide if we should renew it. Bob realized the show was taking too much of his time with no compensation, so he decided it was time to move on.

Starting a radio show was never one of Bob's goals. He

wanted to write, not host a show. He initially got me booked on radio shows because he wanted to share with the public what he had discovered in his first reading. It wasn't like he was getting paid for it; it was more like he couldn't control his passion for it. We then created *The Spirit Communication Hour* because we were both frustrated with the way some radio hosts presented my abilities. Some didn't see what I did as having a spiritual message. They treated me more like a sideshow, a sensational technique for triggering calls from their audience. So Bob found a way for us to produce a radio show on our own.

Being a perfectionist, Bob would spend hours every week preparing for the show. He'd arrive with an outline of questions to ask with points to cover in order to educate the public. But the show was a hobby that was eating up too much of his life, so he knew it was time to move on so he could spend more time writing and making a living. Yet he encouraged me to continue the show on my own. In fact, Bob felt I *should* do the show alone.

The problem was that Bob was the one who got me into radio; I didn't know if I *could* do it on my own. He's the kind of guy who knows how to make things happen. And he's a natural when it comes to marketing and publicity. Therefore, Bob's the kind of guy who is easy to become dependent upon. And he didn't want me to become dependent upon him.

"How am I supposed to do the show without you?" I asked.

"Vicki, you *are* the show," he said, "People are not tuning in to listen to my skeptical remarks. They want to hear messages from spirits. Long after people have forgotten about the guy who used be on the radio with Vicki Monroe, they are going to remember the gal who allowed them to talk with their mother in heaven. It's time you learned to do this alone."

"But I don't know how to use the equipment or lead in and out of the commercials," I protested.

"It's easy," Bob said in a quiet reassuring voice, "Stop your worrying. I know you can do it."

DISCOVERING MY PERSONAL POWER

Once again, I was faced with a terror and anxiety like I had never felt before—unprecedented fear. Not only that, but our contract with the radio station was up for renewal. Yet, when I considered ending the show to move on to bigger and better, I knew I wasn't ready. I also knew I needed to face my fears and do this alone. I closed my eyes, signed the contract for a couple more months and rushed to the post office before I could change my mind. As I heard the envelope drop, I knew I was entering a new phase in my life: self-reliant, confident and fearless. If I could only convince myself that any of it was true.

After the first show on my own, I felt empowered. I faced my fears and got through it fairly effortlessly. Bob and Melissa called the radio control operator who handled the show's calls to root me on. They said I sounded better than ever. I missed the banter of having a co-host, but I loved the intimacy of talking directly to the radio listeners, even between callers. And it worked! The show continued to succeed over the next two months and I proved to myself that I could do it. Bret was proud of me. My mother was proud of me. And even more importantly, I was proud of myself.

Two months later, when my contract was up for renewal again, I now knew it was time to move on. Although the network was national, the audience was not significant. Something inside me told me not to renew, and I trusted that ending the show was the right decision. My intuition proved correct when, about a year after the John Alexandrov show and just months after *The Spirit Communication Hour* ended, I was asked to appear weekly on Q 97.9 FM, a popular morning radio show in Portland, Maine.

The Q 97.9 FM radio show (known as The Q) was the next pinnacle point in my career as a spirit messenger. I got invited as a guest for the show by a shear stroke of good fortune. The Q is a pop station for a younger audience—my children listened to it. And because my little darlings don't shut off lights or radios before they leave for school in the morning, I happened to be listening to The Q when the DJ, Meredith Manning, was asking a trivia question about herbs. Since I had earned my doctorate degree in naturology, I knew the answer. So I decided to call the station, not knowing what I might win.

In my conversation with Meredith, she happened to ask how I knew the answer. I told her I was a naturologist and spirit messenger. The only reason I said both was because the naturology is how I knew the answer, but I now considered my job title as "spirit messenger." Meredith locked onto the spirit messenger part of my answer and started asking me questions. Before I knew it, she was inviting me to be a guest on the show the following Thursday. So I gave her my automatic response, "Yes, I'll do it!"

When I did the morning show on The Q that Thursday, it was a different format than anything I had done before. This was primarily a music station, so I gave readings while the songs were playing, and then, Meredith and Jeff Parsons aired them between songs during all the banter between Meredith, Jeff and myself.

The show went really well and, as destiny would have it, I was asked to come *every* Thursday morning. I was ecstatic because I missed doing a radio show and I really felt comfortable with Meredith and Jeff. They felt more like family members than coworkers. I immediately felt a sister connection with Meredith and knew we had been sisters in a past life. Jeff is one of those unshakable, although lovable, skeptics. And while he felt like a brother, it was more like one of those mischievous little brothers that you just want to throttle sometimes. So the energy between us was perfect for a morning show, and within months, the Thursday show was topping the show's ratings.

MY ULTIMATE FEAR: LIVE ON STAGE

After doing the morning show on The Q for about six months, I felt a desire to reach out to people in a different way. I didn't want to leave The Q; I only wanted to present spirit communication in a way that was different from radio or private readings. I wanted to give the public another option.

Months prior, Bob had talked to me about doing live medium demonstrations on stage where I would randomly give readings to a live audience. At the time, Bob was going to set up and promote these events. Yet, now, Bob and I rarely crossed paths anymore. He was busy writing his book and growing his online magazine, OfSpirit.com. I realized that if I was ever going to offer such an event, I was going to have to plan it, promote it and perform it on my own.

You'd think that everything I had been through so far would have prepared me for any new venture. But a medium demonstration is live! It's one thing to sit behind a microphone and give readings. It is a completely different, and more risky, experience to stand in front of two hundred people and do it! Psychic mediums are not born with a natural ability to speak in front of large crowds. At least, I wasn't. I was like everybody else in this regard—public speaking was my number one fear.

My thoughts immediately jumped to visions of me bombing. I started to panic once again, "What if I don't get any messages? What if I freeze in front of everyone? What if nobody buys a ticket?"

Well, thanks to the growing popularity of The Q's Thursday morning show, selling two hundred tickets was the easy part. Unfortunately, I had never given readings to a large audience before and I didn't know what that would be like. Would spirits even show up? In a crowded room, how would I know which spirit belonged to whom? Although I didn't know the answers to such questions, experience had taught me to trust that it would all work out. I knew other mediums had done it, so I knew it was possible. And, for some reason, I felt compelled to do it. So while I trembled at the thought of my first event, I knew it was something I needed to do.

I called Bob to ask if he'd speak at the event. Upon accepting, he gave me some tips that he learned from attending other psychic medium demonstrations. He also helped me price the tickets, since I had no idea how much to charge. Later, he and Melissa, along with Meredith and her husband, Skip, met with Bret and I at a restaurant a couple times to plan the details of the event. Meredith, my co-host at The Q, agreed to introduce me. Bob would give a speech. And Bret, my mother, my sister, Amy, and some friends agreed to help with decorating, tickets and seating. It helped to know I'd be surrounded by loved-ones at my first medium demonstration.

By this time, about a month before the first event, so many people were calling for tickets that I already had to book another demonstration. The first one sold out about in about five weeks. My mother helped me with ticket sales, mailings and banquet hall arrangements. Bret arranged for security, since he was nervous about who might show up. And Bob wrote me an ad for a local magazine, which he also published on OfSpirit.com. It read:

Contact The Spirit World

"Lessons In The Light" with Dr. Vicki Monroe

Lecture, Questions & Random Audience Readings

Imagine yourself in a ballroom of an old Kennebunkport resort that is lighted entirely by candles. The ocean breeze enters the room through the oversized windows overlooking the water. The candle flames dance and your heart begins to pound. Tonight is not just another lecture about the afterlife, but rather, an interactive experience that will forever change your life. Spirit messenger Vicki Monroe enters the front of the room to answer the questions most people have about her gift and the insight she has gained from it. As she overlooks the audience, she isn't just seeing the guests; she is also seeing the spirits who guide these guests day by day. Tonight, your spirit guides have come hoping to be chosen by Vicki to communicate the messages they have for you. As the evening progresses, the summer sun will fade, but your heart will lighten from the lessons you will learn.

The first event was the toughest because each moment was unexpected, although it went off without a hitch. The messages came through loud and clear. I was horrified before it began, but once I got on stage, I was so focused on the spirits' messages that I forgot about being nervous. I also realized why public speakers and comedians spend their lives on stage. I felt an energy rush from the audience that I had never experienced before. It was like my aura connected with the auras of two hundred people all at the same time. And rather than feel confusion about which spirits belonged to whom, I felt extreme clarity that surely resulted from this energy connection with the audience. And then came another surprise. I also found out I was funny!

You'd never think that an event focused around deceased

friends and relatives could be comically entertaining, but emotions are running so high that one second you're crying and the next second you're laughing. This happens in private readings, too, but not to the same degree as in a public forum. Somehow, sharing that your grandfather had big ears or that your sister in spirit still hates your haircut is comical to people. And while it might not be funny to read, such comments provoke instant laughter from an audience who just balled their eyes out when a deceased father shared with his son (in the audience) the pride he felt for the man he had become. While it requires a prudent sense of timing and cautious discretion to know when and with whom to be funny—both of which I surprisingly understood innately—it is deeply appreciated by the audience in order to make the medium demonstration enjoyable as well as rewarding, rather than a two-hour doggy-downer.

LIFE LESSON: SELF-RELIANCE

The next few years would be filled with new risks and experiences that would challenge my courage and self-confidence, but never so much as the events of this first year-and-a-half as a professional spirit messenger. I have so much to thank Bob for in getting me started using the media to spread my message; but nothing has been more empowering than my own decision to face my fears and do what I felt compelled to do, even when I was frozen in fright. In fact, I have many people to thank for supporting me in the beginning, especially Bret, my mother and my children. Still, as a woman, a mother of four, and a medium during a time when mediums where not so popular, I know now that there is no more important person responsible for my achievements than myself. This may just be my life's most important lesson.

CHAPTER ELEVEN
MEETING OTHER MEDIUMS

By Bob Olson

Take your hands off the steering wheel.

~ *Gary Zukav*

When I first met Vicki and had my life-changing reading with her, I instantly knew I wanted to write my next book about her gift. I anticipated that the entire book would be based around Vicki, since I didn't expect I would ever meet another legitimate medium in my life. I thought it would be easier to get struck by lightning or win the lottery than to meet another genuine spirit messenger.

What I quickly realized was that I wasn't going to dive right into writing the book. I had a lot to learn. Being a cynical skeptic for thirty-five years doesn't prepare you well for writing a book about spirit communication. So rather than writing, I began researching every book, article, interview, and website on psychic mediums, spirit communication and life-after-death. Later, after reading everything I could locate on these subjects, I increased my research to include past-life regression, near-death experience and mixed categories of after-death communication.

I also spent the first year-and-a-half testing Vicki's abilities, interviewing her family, friends and clients, questioning her on how she communicated with spirits and what it felt like to her, and comparing her experiences with those of other mediums whom I had read about in books and articles. After eighteen months of investigation, however, I felt I didn't have enough original material on mediumship in order to write the book. So I threw the unfinished manuscript into a drawer and told Vicki, "I don't feel I have enough here to finish this book. Let's just wait and see what unfolds. In the meantime, I'm going to create an online holistic magazine, and I'll add much of what I've written on that website as articles for people to read."

Vicki was patient with me. She never mentioned it, but I expect she was frustrated that all our time and effort was being shoved into a drawer. A year-and-a-half is a long time to work on one project. Still, she also knew I am a perfectionist by nature, and if I didn't feel I had sufficient original material to complete the book, Vicki knew there was no sense in forcing it.

AN UNEXPECTED PATH

As part of an overall marketing strategy to help Vicki grow professionally, I had created a website, OfSpirit.com, intending she would take it over some day. However, by this time, radio had become so successful for her that she didn't have time to spend working on a website. Plus, I had noticed one day that VickiMonroe.com was available, so she quickly grabbed it and was now using that domain name. Suddenly I found myself with this OfSpirit.com domain name and didn't know what to do with it.

Because I enjoyed website design, I played around with OfSpirit.com and designed it to be a holistic, spiritual and new age magazine. Then, because I enjoy marketing, I did a marketing test to see if there would be any interest from holistic, spiritual and new age businesses and practitioners to advertise on the website. The first test-market results were extremely positive, so I did another test. The second results were even more successful. I knew I was on to something.

I immediately called three people whose opinions I respected: a lawyer, an accountant and a stockbroker. I told them about my test-market results and they all told me the same thing, "Write a business plan and send it to me to look over." It was a little strange that three people all said the same thing, so I created the business plan. It took me seven fourteen-hour days to write it. When it was done, I sent each of my advisors a copy. They all responded by wanting to invest in the company!

I had always been entrepreneurial throughout my life, but I had never considered starting an Internet magazine—especially a holistic magazine. But I pay attention to the way things flow in my life, and when coincidences like this occur, I know I can't ignore them. So I sent the business plan to a few more people, and almost every one of them called me back wanting to invest in OfSpirit.com. It was the most unusual business experience I have ever had. Everything flowed so effortlessly, I have to believe it was all meant to be—just another predestined leg of my journey.

Before I knew it, OfSpirit.com was up and running. Within the first six months, I had win-win business relationships with a major holistic magazine in the New England area, *Spirit of Change* magazine, and a national publisher, AOL Time Warner Book Group, to exchange publicity on OfSpirit.com for content. In almost no time, I had other newsletter, magazine and book publishers who wanted to be part of OfSpirit.com. It all happened so fast that I didn't have the time or employees to handle it all so quickly. Some of these publishers had to wait so I could fully maximize what we had already manifested.

Early in OfSpirit.com's growth, I was diligent to get practitioners to write articles about their expertise. Today, numerous authors, publishers, writers and practitioners send us articles daily; but nobody knew about us back then. So I was calling practitioners on the telephone telling them about the Internet magazine and inviting them to write for it. It was another win-win relationship since the practitioner would get publicity by adding a bio at the end of their article while we got educational content written by experts in their field for our visitors to read.

By this time, Vicki had stumbled upon a new gig at The Q—an FM radio station in Portland, Maine—and was keeping herself busy with a long waiting list of readings. I was working eighteen-hour days to get OfSpirit.com up and running. So, resultantly, Vicki and I had little contact with one another during this time. In hindsight, it is clear that this was all meant to be, because now that I wasn't focused on one psychic medium, several more came into my life.

SEEKING ARTICLES BUT DISCOVERING MEDIUMS

This part of my journey began when one holistic practitioner I knew gave me a list of practitioners she knew whom I could call to obtain articles for OfSpirit.com. One of these practitioners was a psychic medium. When I contacted this medium, my phone call was solely out of desperation for website content and not related to my research for a book. The book was still in a drawer, and I had no intention—or time—to begin my research again. The morning I called this medium, I only half blurted out my speech about needing articles when he interrupted me.

"What is your name again?" he asked.

"Bob Olson," I said.

"Bob," he said, "I'm going to be honest with you, I'm not very familiar with the Internet, and really not interested in buying advertising right now..."

I wanted to say that I wasn't calling to sell advertising. I wanted to say that I was seeking practitioners who wrote articles, that I didn't even have anything to *sell* at this point, but the medium wasn't in the mood for listening. He told me he was with clients and didn't have time to talk. I wondered to myself why he answered the phone in the first place if he was with clients. I later learned that he almost never answers the phone while with a client. I guess our meeting was meant to be. There were forces at work that were beyond my understanding.

"Even though I'm not interested in your Internet advertising, Bob, I think I have a message for you. Is your father deceased?" he said.

I half wanted to make him understand that I wasn't calling to sell Internet advertising, but the other half of me didn't have the energy. It was obvious he didn't understand, and now he had mentioned my father. Since my father was a strong communicator and was always there when Vicki received messages from the other side, it really didn't surprise me that Dad might come through—that is, if this medium was in fact legitimate. Since Vicki and I hadn't talked in a while, I wondered if my father might be trying to contact me in a new way.

"Yes," I said, "my father has passed."

"Well, he's here with me now, and he was coming through

last night during a group session I gave at my home. He kept giving me your name, but when I asked the group if anyone knew you, your name didn't sound familiar to anyone. Now I understand why I was getting it; your father knew you would be calling this morning and wanted me to pay attention to it."

I laughed, partly because my father cracks me up the way he does things, partly because the whole situation was a little bizarre. "I don't know how my father knew I was going to call you," I said, "I didn't even know I was going to call you until this morning. I'm just calling names on a list."

"People in the spirit world can see a little into the future," the medium explained. "Your father knew you would be calling. He has an important message for you, but I'm with clients right now so I'll call you in two or three days, okay?"

I must have had one of those really stupid looks on my face, because my jaw dropped and my mouth was open due to the shock of what this medium just did to me. Nevertheless, he seemed really rushed so I just said, "Okay, I'll talk to you in two or three days."

SCATTERBRAIN OR SCAM ARTIST?

It wasn't that I was all that shocked that my father came through—I was no longer surprised by spirit communication—it was that the medium told me that my father had an "important" message for me but then said he wouldn't call me back for two or three days! If I had been anyone else, I might have freaked out thinking all sorts of terrible stuff. What's the important message my father's spirit has for me? Am I dying? Is someone I know dying? Am I in danger? Is someone I know in danger? Those are some of the first thoughts that would go through most people's minds if they heard their father was trying to get an "important" message to them from the *other side*.

I got off the phone and walked into the office to tell Melissa what had just occurred. Her immediate reaction was one of concern. "What do you think the important message is? What do you mean we have to wait two or three days!" She was a little perturbed.

I just laughed. "Honey, if my father had anything important to tell us, don't you think he could just tell Vicki?"

"I don't know," she said, "We haven't talked to her in a couple weeks. Maybe we should call her."

"No, I'm not going to bother Vicki. That's silly. I'm sure it's nothing. Just forget about it for now. We'll know in two or three days."

Melissa wasn't comforted by my aloofness, but how else was I going to deal with the situation? After all, it *was* kind of funny. But as the day passed, I realized there was an important lesson here for the medium that he needed to learn, so I called him the next day and explained to him the implications of what he did. He was much less rushed this time. He apologized and we set an appointment for a reading.

I realized that this would be a great way for a scam artist to get clients: telling people their loved ones in spirit have an important message for them but that they must make an appointment to get the message. On the other hand, I also knew that this medium might just be having one of those scatterbrain moments to which we can all relate. But I accepted the risk of getting ripped off, trusting that there also might be a divine purpose behind all this. It turned out that the medium was legitimate and was just a little overwhelmed at the time.

The "important" information my father had for me was

that I was doing the right thing by starting the magazine. My father explained that he was with me every step of the way; that he had helped me attract investors and business relationships; that he was proud of me; and that OfSpirit.com was going to be very successful. While this message was very meaningful to me, I now believe that my father was really just leading me to meet another psychic medium.

DISCOVERING A THIRD, FOURTH... AND TWENTY-FIFTH MEDIUM

In my continued efforts to seek articles, I soon contacted another medium that I found listed in a holistic directory I was using to contact practitioners. Just as with the last psychic medium, I didn't give any thought to the fact that he was a medium and I was writing a book on mediumship. OfSpirit.com was now eating every waking hour of my life and all I wanted at this moment in my life was articles. I hoped this medium would have something I could use on the *Psychics & Mediums* page.

The medium said he didn't have much interest in writing, but he offered to be interviewed if that would help. Since I was working from eight in the morning until two in the morning to get OfSpirit.com off the ground, I didn't have time to interview him and write an article. But after talking with him on the phone, I really liked the guy; so Melissa and I ended up meeting him for dinner one weekend night. We all hit it off immediately and have been great friends ever since.

This medium turned out to be a catalyst for my introduction to another medium. This psychic medium, a woman, introduced me to several other mediums—as many as three in one day. And then these mediums introduced me to still more mediums. After my first year as editor-in-chief of OfSpirit.com, I had met some twenty-five psychic mediums from around the world, including mediums from Scotland and England.

One Monday, I happened to be talking to one new medium I had met about his gift of spirit communication. We were having one of those truth-seeking conversations where time zips by like a bicycle courier in the city. I think a couple hours had passed when he started telling me about a medium he heard about who had an unusual talent.

"I don't know her name," he said, "but she can draw the spirit she is communicating with right there during the reading. I would love to have that gift. It would be so validating for my clients to be able to take that drawing home with them."

I had heard about this woman before, but I had never met her. I was intrigued, and I had a feeling I'd be meeting this unusually talented medium some day. Two days later, another medium I know called me on the phone.

"Bob, I'm calling to invite you to come see my friend give a lecture and demonstration on Easter Sunday at [a Spiritualist church]. She's from England and has a different style of mediumship that is very unique to English mediums. I think you'd enjoy it if you could come," she said.

I was intrigued to see an English medium work, but Melissa and I had plans to get together with my mother and sister on Easter. I told the woman about those plans, but explained that I didn't know what time we were getting together. "What time does the service begin?" I asked her.

"It's from eleven to one. But, Bob, I don't want you to mess up your plans with your family. Why don't I just give you the pastor's phone number at the church? If it turns out you can come, you can call her for directions. You've probably heard of her... she's the medium who draws people's spirit-guides."

This is one of those coincidences that I know exists to get my attention. If I hadn't just heard about this woman two days prior, I may never have given the Easter service a second thought. But now I knew I was supposed to go, so I wasn't surprised on Friday when my mother told me that she and my sister were sick with the flu.

"Would you mind if we didn't get together on Easter, Bob?" my mother asked, "Even if we are feeling better on Sunday, we should continue to rest for a couple days."

Sometimes the path is so clear you can see the future.

OH, I GET IT, THE BOOK IS WRITING ITSELF

In an effort to remember my experiences, I began writing about each of these "coincidental" events. I finally caught on that the Universe was guiding me to these mediums, so I began documenting my experiences in writing and publishing these writings on OfSpirit.com. It wasn't long before people all over the world began reading what I wrote and emailing me with messages of gratitude for sharing my experiences. My first reading experience with Vicki—Chapter Three in this book—was one of those articles.

About four months after starting OfSpirit.com, a magazine editor read my article about my first reading with Vicki and approached me about reprinting it in her magazine. On the first day it hit the stands, people started calling both Vicki and me. Vicki's clientele instantly grew from a waiting list of three months to about ten months. And I was constantly bombarded with letters and phone calls from readers who thanked me for sharing my experience with them. At that point in my career, it was one of the most touching experiences I had ever had in relation to my writing.

I started to realize that when I first began my research

with Vicki, I thought I was writing a book. Now it was obvious that the book was writing itself. The best thing I ever did was to stop trying to control my research and just let things happen.

Although I didn't understand it to the depth that I do today, I was beginning to think that I am not really the person at the steering wheel of my life. Perhaps a Higher Power is in the driver's seat and I'm only along for the ride. Once I finally accepted this idea, my life progressed much more smoothly and was a heck of a lot more fun. Every morning I'd wake up and say, "I wonder what today is going to bring!" I wasn't always thrilled with the results, but I was never bored.

My research into mediumship had now taken a new direction. Most mediums I met gave me a private reading and I watched some give medium demonstrations on stage in front of live audiences. I was immediately intrigued by both the parallels and the discrepancies between mediums. I loved comparing how they linked with spirits and how they delivered their messages. It surprised me how mediums from all over the world basically used the same methods, yet nobody was born with a training manual for their gift. I quickly realized that I could learn a great deal about mediumship by studying large numbers of mediums, especially since Vicki had provided me with such a solid foundation on which to compare them all.

I was also introduced to a religion I never knew existed, Spiritualism. I didn't join a Spiritualist church, but I was fascinated by how different it was from the Catholic Church in which I was raised. In fact, the Spiritualist churches usually had pastors who were psychic mediums. And they trained people who recognized their own gift of mediumship but didn't know how to develop it or use it properly. It was a religion that made more sense to me than any I had previously recognized, but I wasn't looking to join a church. I felt content seeking my truth without the issues that come with joining a church, association or group.

The Spiritualist Church introduced me to the "medium circle," a group of psychic mediums who gather regularly to practice their mediumistic skills. Sometimes churches are the center-point for such groups, but not always. Many mediums whom are not involved in a church are either part of a circle or simply part of a group of mediums that congregate, study and meet together often.

THE DARK TRUTH ABOUT MEDIUMS: THEY ARE HUMAN

At first I saw this as a wonderful opportunity for new mediums who needed mentoring. And it does serve that purpose well. But, like any group dynamic, it often has its issues. What I found most surprising and displeasing among such groups was a competitiveness and clique-iness between and among the mediums. This, of course, wasn't true of every group or every medium in a group, but it was common enough to disturb me more than once.

I guess I was misguided in thinking that psychic mediums were above such pettiness because their gift fell into the spiritual category. I wanted to believe that God would only give the most spiritual of humans such an incredible gift. But once the newness of my relationships with mediums settled, I usually got an inside look at the personal struggles and complicated group dynamics of these extraordinary people. Sometimes the view was in line with what I wanted to see. Other times, the landscape I observed was disconcerting.

I was at first shocked to learn that there lived a jealousy in some mediums for the success or recognition of other mediums in their circle. One medium was dubbed "Best Psychic" in a city magazine, only to have so-called friends from her own peer group send a letter to the magazine setting the editors straight that better mediums existed in the city.

Later, I witnessed and heard about bickering, verbal back-stabbing and even public displays of competitive squabbling among mediums at events, health fairs, mediumship development workshops, and of course, via the telephone. I was appalled by such conduct from people I held in such high esteem. Oh, don't get me wrong; I'm not saying that *most* mediums are like this. Such conduct was of a minority, not a majority. I was simply stunned to witness it at all. And it was a lesson that I undoubtedly needed to learn.

The negative conduct I witnessed with some mediums had me shouting "YUCK!" to the whole idea of writing a book about these gifted people. I threw the manuscript back into a drawer, promising myself to bury this part of me forever. I felt deflated. It had all started off so good. My experience with Vicki had been positive and inspiring and had me wanting to share what I learned with the world. But now, how could I write about mediumship when it seemed so shrouded with conflict and negativity. So I set the book aside, once again, expecting I may never return to it.

With time, I processed the lessons to be gained from this new perspective of psychic mediums. I realized I needed to recognize that there are different personalities and intents behind this amazing gift. Just because the gift deals with spirits does not mean the medium is, by default, spiritual. If truth be told, after four years of dealing with hundreds of psychic mediums, some of the most unspiritual people I have ever met are mediums. On the other hand, some of the most spiritual people I have ever met are mediums, too. In the end, it means only one thing: mediums are people just like the rest of us. And once I fully understood this lesson, I wrote an article titled, *"Mediums Are People, Too!"* and published it on OfSpirit.com. It concludes with the following passage:

"Mediums are no different than the rest of us. They have a gift but so do pianists and painters and teachers and hairdressers and accountants. We all have something we are good at, something that sets us apart from the crowd. Just because a medium's gift seems to fall within the spiritual realm of human abilities, that does not make them any more enlightened or spiritual than you or me. The artist's and musician's gifts are also incredibly spiritual, but we don't hold them up as enlightened beings. And we don't expect them to be all-knowing or perfect. We shouldn't place these expectations upon mediums either. Mediums are people, too. And as someone who knows many gifted mediums, I must admit that it is their human qualities that make them most special."

This experience also taught me to value mediums who use their gift with the utmost integrity, purest intent and with the highest degree of responsibility. After getting to know which mediums had the most extraordinary gifts, as well as which fell in line with my desired standards of integrity, intent and responsibility, I learned to appreciate such mediums so much that I created a website, BestPsychicMediums.com, to tell the world about them. Vicki, of course, was the first to be included on that list. I call it my *"Genuine & Legitimate Psychic Mediums List."*

CHAPTER TWELVE
DIFFERENCES & DISCREPANCIES
BETWEEN MEDIUMS

By Bob Olson

Living is a form of not being sure, not knowing what next or how. The moment you know how, you begin to die a little. The artist never entirely knows. We guess. We may be wrong, but we take leap after leap in the dark.

~ *Agnes de Mille*

One benefit to exploring the gifts of more than one medium comes from recognizing the differences and discrepancies between them. Early in my research, I was excited by the parallels among mediums regarding how they worked and what they taught. Later, I was surprised to notice how often mediums differ in what they say and do. This chapter discusses some of those differences and discrepancies, and reveals the lessons these dissimilarities teach us.

SAME QUESTION, DIFFERENT ANSWERS

Whether it's a live medium demonstration with Vicki Monroe, a television demonstration with John Edward or a private reading with James Van Praagh, mediums are almost always asked questions about the afterlife. And in almost every case, the medium provides an answer. So what are we supposed to believe when three or four mediums answer the same question differently?

I first realized there were some discrepancies between mediums when I was reading books written by famous mediums like George Anderson, Sylvia Browne, John Edward and James Van Praagh, to name just a few. Later, I heard these inconsistencies among several mediums I interviewed in person. One of the key issues mediums do not agree on is suicide. Many people want to know what happens to a person when they commit suicide. Well, ask three different mediums and you could get three different answers.

Most mediums agree that there is no hell, except for what we mentally create for ourselves here on earth. So there is agreement that suicide victims do not go to hell. But one medium says that suicide victims return to another earthly life immediately to accomplish what they originally planned to do. Another medium claims that suicide victims lie in a dormant state of limbo for a period of time, almost as though they are sleeping off a bad hangover. Another claims that people who commit suicide must wait out the life they took (their own) until it was supposed to be over, as though they lie waiting in regret while watching their loved-ones go through that life without them. And finally, most mediums will tell you that you go into the light and love of the spirit world like everyone else—possibly under the care of special souls who help suicide victims—but with deep regret for cutting short the learning opportunity you had hoped for before entering that life. I believe in the latter version, but the different versions vary so much that it is confusing to know exactly what to believe.

MEDIUMS ARE LIMITED IN THEIR KNOWLEDGE ABOUT THE AFTERLIFE

What these inconsistencies teach us is that mediums don't have all the answers. They are limited in their knowledge of the afterlife in two ways: One, they are limited by their own human ability to understand infinite principles; and Two, they are limited by their own subjective perceptions.

Spirits teach us that the brilliancy of the colors, the striking beauty of the music and loving warmth of the light in the spirit world are unlike anything we can imagine here on earth. Some of you are probably asking yourself, "There is light and music in the spirit world?" Who among us really knows? Whatever spirits are experiencing in their world is apparently indescribable using our human language and understanding. Therefore, spirits use points of reference that we can understand, like describing the light as "the sun," to give us some idea of what they are experiencing.

When spirits try to explain these unexplainable things to a medium, they will use points of reference meaningful to each individual medium to convey the most accurate description possible. A description that might work for one medium won't necessarily fit the mental framework of another medium. Hence, we get confusion and discrepancies between what mediums know about the afterlife.

I wish more mediums would refrain from answering certain questions about the afterlife. My frustration lies in knowing that individuals and audiences hearing or reading their answers often take what these mediums say verbatim. Many people will even argue about something they heard or read from a medium as if it were God's truth. It is true that some mediums know a lot more about the afterlife than most people; but again, what they know is filtered by their own perceptions and points of reference. I believe they should acknowledge this before answering questions.

There are some inconsistencies among mediums that are unexplainable, and not very important either. I read from one medium's book that people in the spirit world are *all* thirty years old. Other mediums tell me that spirits show themselves as they felt best while here on earth—that could be at age twenty, thirty, or even sixty. Perhaps mediums should stick to answering these types of questions by saying, "In my experience, this is what it's like in the spirit world..." Apparently, different mediums have different experiences in the way spirits show themselves, including the ages in which spirits appear.

MEDIUMS DON'T KNOW WHAT THEY DON'T KNOW—EXPERIENCE IS SUBJECTIVE

Why do mediums give answers to questions that are in disagreement with other mediums? In most cases, the medium doesn't know his or her answer is in disagreement with that of another medium. Most mediums are not comparing notes. Even if they did, they might not realize their answer is different. It would be like two people describing what the color blue looks like or what a pear tastes like. We don't go around asking other people how they experience blue or pears. So how do we know if our experience is the same as that of other people? In short, mediums don't know what they don't know.

I remember learning in college as a criminology major that five people can witness the same crime at the exact same moment and at the exact same location, yet give five different versions of what happened in their witness statements. Are they lying? No. They are simply describing the crime the way *they* saw it. Who is right and who is wrong? We can never really know. Even if the criminal returned to confess his version of the story, his individual perspective would also taint his description of what happened.

NEAR-DEATH EXPERIENCES ALSO DIFFER

There is a chapter in this book that explains how "knowing" comes from personal experience, not from vicarious experience (not from hearing about someone else's experience). This is also true when it comes to understanding the afterlife. In studying information on Near-Death Experiences (when people die but return back to life), I noticed many similarities in people's descriptions about their death experience. However, the inconsistencies among people's descriptions were often based on their subjective spiritual frame of reference (spiritual beliefs, religion and personal points of reference).

Many people during their near-death experience were soon met by a "greeter" after leaving their body. For some, this is described as a white being of light or an all-knowing light. Others say it is a bright ball of love. Some describe it as a relative, friend or guide from the spirit world—even a deceased pet. Still others describe it as a spiritual being, Buddha, Mohammed, Jesus or God. The variations of details were many; the basic concept was the same. There is little question that these people have described similar experiences; they were all met by a "greeter." It was their subjective contexts that altered the particulars.

EACH MEDIUM'S GIFT MAY WORK A LITTLE DIFFERENTLY

There is also another reason for the differences in how mediums answer questions: *each medium's gift may work a little differently.*

For the first year and a half into my research, I would often call Vicki to ask her questions. I got used to the way her gift worked and assumed most other mediums worked the same way. About a year later, I was talking to another exceptionally gifted medium and decided to ask him a question.

"Two days ago," I said, "I was sitting in my bedroom and had an overwhelming sense that a spirit was in the room with me. I actually felt like this spirit was trying to get a message to me, but I had no intuitive sense of who it might be. Can you get anything on who it was or what the message was about?" I asked.

"Sorry, Bob, it doesn't work that way," he said. "If you had called me two days ago while it was happening, I might have got something, but not now. I can't look into the past, you know," he laughed.

At first I felt embarrassed for asking such a naïve question. Then, after I hung up the phone, I realized that I shouldn't feel embarrassed because Vicki had been doing this for me ever since I met her. With Vicki, she would know who I was talking about immediately because the spirit would show up in front of her the second I brought it up, telling her what they wanted to convey to me at couple days prior. If I was wrong, and there wasn't anyone trying to give me a message, then nobody would show up when I mentioned it to Vicki. She would say, "Either you don't need the message anymore or there wasn't anyone trying to communicate with you, because nobody is claiming to have been there that day."

What this other medium may not have realized was that "his" gift does not work this way, or at least he *thinks* it doesn't. This gifted medium wasn't telling me false information; he was telling me true information based on his personal point of reference—how his own gift works.

Aside from the fact that some mediums see spirits, some hear them, some communicate telepathically and some do all of the above, there are also differences in how, when and where their gifts work. Some of these differences, however, might have more to do with the medium's belief system than the actually reality of the situation. I believe that this medium actually does have the ability to answer the question I had above, but he "believes" he can't and is therefore limited to that reality. Perhaps he had a teacher or mentor who passed this limiting message on to him.

Most experienced mediums have learned to turn their gift off while not working. It is a useful strategy to conserve their energy this way. The gift is always there in the background, like a radio they can hear in the other room, but they keep the volume down low when they are not working so they can maximize their efforts when they are working. So when I asked the medium above about the spirit who was coming to me two days prior, his gift wasn't turned on for him to know if anyone was there with a message for me. Because he didn't "believe" his gift works this way, he never turned it on to see if it could.

Vicki, on the other hand, already had her gift turned on whenever we worked together, so this wouldn't have been an issue for her. She was used to turning it on before I interviewed her or spoke with her on the phone. Plus, she believed her gift *did* work that way—nobody had ever told her otherwise—so she would have turned it on even if it were off to see if someone was there with a message for me.

BELIEFS MAY AFFECT A MEDIUM'S ABILITIES

When a medium from Scotland spoke at a psychic development workshop I attended for beginners, he told us how he studied mediumship for seven years with some of the best mediums in history. Then he admitted having to unlearn most of what he had learned. He said this took him another seven years to shed all the limiting beliefs he had acquired from his mentors and the books he had studied. It was an interesting testament to what I had been witnessing with some of the mediums I had researched and/or met.

Mediums are human, so they grow and stretch their abilities just like the rest of us. Many of us are limited in our abilities because of the limiting beliefs we have about what we can do. How many people believe they can't draw, can't sing or can't juggle only to learn one day that they are mistaken? I often hear stories about people discovering an unknown talent for painting or drawing years into adulthood. Mediums are no different.

MEDIUMS HELPS US MAKE OUR OWN INTERPRETATIONS

I don't believe mediums have their gift to teach us exactly what it is like in the spirit world. They can give us a clue, but they don't know for sure. No one will truly know what the spirit world is like until we get there. Even those people who seem to have gone there and returned in their near-death experiences will admit that it is terribly difficult to explain something so infinite, sacred and divine using our limited vocabulary.

Mediums can, however, help us gain evidence that an afterlife exists. They certainly can help us know that our loved-ones continue to exist and are happy, alive and pain-free despite their physical death here on earth. Perhaps, however, we should stop asking them questions beyond that, or else risk confusion and misunderstandings. Perhaps we should remember that mediums are *not* all-knowing enlightened beings, but rather, human beings with an extraordinary ability to communicate with spirits and connect with their advanced senses. We shouldn't confuse their spiritual gift with God-like spiritual infallibility or omniscience. We should see mediums as human and allow them to be the "spiritual beings having a human experience" that we all are. With this understanding, we can take what these mediums teach us based on their own individual experiences to determine our own truths and beliefs about living, dying and the afterlife. In essence, we can use our studies and experiences for understanding spirit as a catalyst toward understanding ourselves.

PART V
Does Everyone Have The Gift Of Mediumship?

CHAPTER THIRTEEN
A PSYCHIC & MEDIUMSHIP
DEVELOPMENT WORKSHOP

By Bob Olson

Our deepest fear is not that we are inadequate. Our deepest fear is that we are powerful beyond measure.

~ Marianne Williamson

One of the most common questions asked of mediums is if everyone has the ability to communicate with spirits the way they do. I have heard a lot of mediums answer yes to this question, but I think it is out of a need to avoid sounding egotistic. That is a loaded question if you think about it. If they answer that we don't all have the ability, then they appear egotistical. If they answer that we do all have the ability, then they are answering the question without really thinking it through or without providing a thorough answer.

A GIFTED ABILITY LIKE MUSIC OR ART

The fact is that we *do* all have the ability to communicate with spirit, just like we all have the ability to paint pictures and play the piano. But some people are going to paint like Picasso and play the piano like Amadeus while the rest of us will be painting clowns by number and playing Chopsticks on the piano.

Mediumship is a gift, much like art or music. I could learn to play the piano fairly well with years of practice, but I'm never going to be a concert pianist. That's the difference between "learning" how to be a medium and naturally having the gift. Psychic mediums like Vicki are naturals. Some have studied to improve their gift, but most have known of their unique abilities since childhood. Before many of them ever read a book about psychic mediumship, they were giving readings to friends and coworkers the way some people show others their latest card trick.

With that said, I have been to workshops that teach mediumship where a few students have discovered an impressive, and unexpected, ability to connect with spirit. While some gifted individuals know they have unusual psychic abilities, they often don't realize just how gifted they are, or how to use it. It is not uncommon that someone will attend one of these workshops and discover a hidden talent of which they were not fully aware. But we must keep in mind that these people were not *totally* unaware of their gift; they were drawn to the workshop for a reason.

I once attended a workshop offered by a psychic medium from Scotland. I didn't go intending to discover any profound ability in myself—in fact, I really stunk at it—but I was curious to see how other beginners would rate. I was quite surprised by what took place.

A PSYCHIC & MEDIUMSHIP DEVELOPMENT WORKSHOP

The workshop was presented at a Spiritualist Church on a Wednesday evening. About forty people attended. The teacher took us through several workshop experiments to test our abilities. The first was an exercise where we attempted to learn something about a stranger (our workshop partner) by picking up information through their aura. I was astounded at how well some people did. One attendee picked up on his partner's childhood trauma, another on her partner's honeymoon memories, and a third on her partner's work related problems. *My* mind went completely blank. The best I could hope for was that my partner had no past, but that wasn't the case.

The second exercise involved psychometry. Attendees would hold something personal that belonged to a perfect stranger—like a watch, piece of jewelry or a scarf—and they would see what information they could pick up from that object. Dawn, the girl who held my watch, said it was a gift I had given to myself in celebration of something, but that it no longer held the importance it once had when I first bought it. Not bad, I thought. The watch was a gift that Melissa and I had purchased in celebration of overcoming a five-year depression. The watch had lost its significance to me because, at the time, it had been over seven years since I overcame that horrible depression and I was allowing myself to move on from it after having made peace with that growth experience in my life.

Finally, the teacher tried our hands at mediumship. I happened to get paired up with a guy named Craig for this exercise. I didn't know Craig personally, but I knew he was a healer at the church. When Melissa and I visited this church one Easter to see a guest medium from England, Craig was a healer there who surprised Melissa by causing her eyelids to flutter uncontrollably for about ten minutes while he held her shoulders and meditated to give her healing energy. Craig wasn't a medium, but had been offering his healing gift to the church for years. The night of this workshop, Craig told me that he came to the workshop to see if he might have *mediumship* abilities, as well.

AN EYE FLUTTERING, FINGER TWITCHING PERFORMANCE

Craig was the first to give mediumship an effort; I would go second. When the teacher gave the signal to start, Craig sat with his hands palms-up on his knees. This isn't how most mediums work—most mediums just start talking—but Craig was obviously using his healing meditation methods to connect with spirit. I think it was the best way he knew to clear his conscious thoughts. Next, Craig's eyelids began fluttering the way Melissa had described of her own eyelids on Easter. Then his fingers started twitching as if he was getting shock treatments. He sat like this for a few minutes while I waited and watched.

To our side was an experienced medium who was rattling off messages from spirit to one of the workshop attendees. The woman was the odd-man-out when everybody paired up, so the medium—who was only there to watch the workshop—sat across from her so she wouldn't have to miss the exercise. I thought to myself how intimidating it must be for Craig to be sitting there in complete silence while this experienced medium was relaying messages like an auctioneer. It didn't seem to affect Craig. In fact, he was so silent and still—except for his eyelids and fingers—that I wondered if we lost him in the cosmos somewhere.

Slowly and peacefully, Craig opened his eyes. His fingers stopped twitching. He told me he had linked with a man in spirit. I thought to myself, jokingly, "Sure you did Craig; and I'm Superman." I figured he was getting caught up in the moment. Then he gave me some unexpected messages.

"The man here has a ruddy complexion. He's rugged looking. He's wearing a plaid flannel shirt. I don't know who he is to you, but he is sitting beside you to your left with a hand on your shoulder," said Craig.

I wasn't sure whether to get excited or not. I knew that this would probably be my father if it were anybody at all. He certainly fit the description, even the plaid flannel shirt was about all my father would ever wear. But this was pretty vague information so far. I just listened without saying anything. Craig didn't wait for me to respond; he went back into trance for thirty or forty seconds with more eye-fluttering and finger-twitching.

When he opened his eyes again, Craig said, " He's telling me he had a problem with alcoholism. He's very sad for what that did to you." Right there I knew it was my father. This is a message my father sends me every time I get a reading, beginning with my very first reading. I keep telling my father that I forgive him for the alcoholism, but this is either an issue my father continues to struggle with or a signal for me to identify him as the spirit coming through.

"He's very emotional," said Craig, visibly feeling choked up by my father's emotion. "I think he died about four or five years ago," he added. That was correct. I was now really impressed that this newcomer to mediumship was so accurate on his first attempt. "He is still sitting beside you. I don't know why, but he is down low to your side." Craig quickly went back into trance as if to ask my father why he was showing himself so low to my side.

Craig opened his eyes again. "He has a hand on your shoulder. He tells me he is down low to your side to represent how he looked up to you while he was here. He says the two of you changed roles sometimes. Does that make sense?" Craig asked.

It did make sense. My father suffered with severe depressions that led him to self-medicate with alcohol. We changed roles because of my father's alcoholism. Sometimes I had to be the adult even though I was a teenager because my father had reduced himself to a vulnerable child drowning in a sea of despair and confusion. As I sat with Craig, I recalled a recurring scene in my family's dining room as my father soaked his white t-shirt in tears. He would plead with me to help him, to forgive him, to understand that he loved me even when his words or actions hadn't indicated love. I would hold him for what seemed like hours while he sobbed, me balling along with him. He was lost. I was bewildered. And while Mom was working to pay the bills, I played adult trying to release the pressure of my father's burdens and fears, comforting him during the darkest stage of his illness—the cry for help. I held an arm around Dad as he dialed one alcohol rehabilitation hospital after another, begging them to admit him one more time. With each refusal, my father's hope and presence diminished. When someone finally offered to admit him, we both sighed in exhaustion and relief, then rushed him to the hospital to detoxify.

My father eventually did stop drinking for twelve years before he died at the age of sixty-three. I was proud of him for that accomplishment. So it was difficult for me to understand why he tortured himself endlessly in the spirit world with memories of his drinking years. But, needless to say, I knew what Craig was talking about. Dad's message was loud and clear, and I didn't question that Craig had linked with him in spirit.

I told Craig that the messages he gave made a lot of sense.

I explained that my father had often come through in readings with that same message, and that I wished he could get over his guilt and move on. I said that my entire family had forgiven my father a long time ago, and it was sad and unfortunate that he keep torturing himself. Craig said he would give my father that message. He quickly went back into trance.

After one more eye-fluttering finger-twitching moment of silence, Craig came back to consciousness. He had a gentle smile on his lips. He was so calm and peaceful, I felt relaxed just being near him.

"I told your father what you said," Craig told me. "He was sitting low by your side. I'm sure he heard you say it yourself. Then two angels came down and took your father by each arm. They lifted him up so he was above you, not below. It was a beautiful vision. I believe your father heard your forgiveness this time. I think it helped him."

I could tell that Craig was moved by what just happened. Whatever he witnessed must have been spectacular because his entire being was glowing. It was now my turn to give mediumship a go. I decided to try Craig's method and do a little meditation to get started.

A LOG ON A STAGE

I closed my eyes and attempted to clear my thoughts. I could hear everyone around me giving messages to their workshop partners. I felt like a log on a stage. My mind was blank as Craig waited patiently for a message from beyond. I wondered how long I should sit there teasing him with anticipation. I felt bad for Craig that he got me as a partner. All I could think about was how well he did linking with my father. I thanked my father for coming through so clearly. I contemplated the effect this night might have on Craig, knowing that he would likely become a powerful medium one day.

After about a minute, I opened my eyes and said, "I'm way too excited about what you just did to be able to do this myself. Have you ever tried mediumship before?" I don't think Craig cared that I sucked at mediumship. I think he was pretty excited about his performance, too. He told me that this was his first time, although he had been learning about mediumship for over a year. I guess he just never tried it before. For the next ten minutes I interviewed Craig like a reporter. I told him how I had been studying mediums for a couple years and that his performance was quite impressive. Then I encouraged him to continue improving his gift with practice.

SAME SPIRIT, DIFFERENT MOOD

Melissa's partner didn't do too shabby either. She told Melissa that she had a sixth sense for predicting bad omens in her life. She had an inner knowing (premonition) that she was going to get into a car accident and, a short time later, it happened. She had an inner knowing that a certain man was going to attack her and it happened. Later, she had the same feeling about another man and he, too, attacked her. Finally, she had an inner knowing that her stepmother was dying and that turned out to come true as well. The woman explained that the car accident and personal attacks happened because she didn't trust her inner knowing and walked right into these dangerous situations despite her premonitions. Now she wanted to learn to trust her gift and discover how to use it for more positive things, not just the bad stuff.

At first Melissa's partner had no success linking with spirit. Melissa thought it might help if she thought of my father, knowing he was a strong communicator from the other side. She wondered if her partner would pick up on his energy as she thought about him. Without telling her partner who she was thinking about, it worked! The woman immediately picked up on my father's energy. This was at the same time that Craig was linking with my father, too.

Okay, time for a quick lesson. Spirits can be in more than one place at one time. I know this is hard to understand for some people, but it is true. Someone in the spirit world can be in an infinite number of places at any given moment. So my father could be with me, Melissa, and even my mother and my sister all at the same time.

People who have had near-death experiences claim to have been in several places at once while they were officially dead for a few minutes. One woman, as portrayed in Dr. Raymond Moody's video *Life After Life*, said she was in her hospital room overlooking the doctors trying to revive her, in the hospital's hallway listening to her brother-in-law talking, and at her sister's home across the country watching her sister look for her car keys—all at the same time. After the woman was revived and feeling better, she was able to verify everything she had heard while officially dead: exactly what the doctors were saying at the time she had flat-lined, the exact words her brother-in-law had spoken in the hallway, and the exact events her sister had experienced while looking for her car keys that day.

Melissa's partner told her she was getting an older man who was old enough to be Melissa's father, but she knew from an earlier exercise that Melissa's father was still alive. This confused the woman because she said the man was too young to be Melissa's grandfather but she was getting a fatherly energy from him. Since I'd been with Melissa since we were kids, my father loved her as his daughter. A few mediums have told me during my own readings that my father always shows Melissa as one of his children; and to my humorous delight, this always confuses the mediums.

Melissa's partner described my father as having gray hair and a button-down plaid shirt with a collar. She added that my father was showing himself with his arm around Melissa and a smile on his face. She said he made her feel happy and was joking with her. This was contrary to the introduction Craig was getting from my father at that same moment, but it was a side to my father that most other mediums have experienced.

My father is ecstatic in the spirit world and enjoying himself immensely. He always jokes around during my readings saying that he was too serious in his earthly life and is now making up for those gloomy years. Although he would become emotional when talking about his years of alcoholism or my five-year depression, the rest of his messages always had a comedic twist that kept the mediums smiling and laughing.

SWAPPING STORIES AND DRAWING CONCLUSIONS

You can probably imagine our surprise when Melissa and I swapped stories on the ride home from the workshop that night. I found the fact that my father came through to both beginner mediums in two completely different moods a rather curious occurrence. We can only speculate on the reason he did this; I really don't know why. Even more significant was the fact that both of our partners linked with spirit. For a beginner's workshop, that was unlikely. My conclusion? Never underestimate anyone's ability to communicate with spirit.

Even if Melissa's partner and Craig never improve their abilities enough to become mediums by profession, they are still several steps above painting by number or playing Chopsticks. I've heard many people say that their art or music talent isn't good enough to make a living from it but the exercise in itself has personal benefits that are priceless. I'm sure Craig and that woman left the workshop that night feeling they would have paid thousands of dollars for that experience. If you have never had your own experience linking with spirit, perhaps you don't have a natural gift of mediumship. But then again... maybe you do.

CHAPTER FOURTEEN
AN ALTERNATE METHOD OF SPIRIT
COMMUNICATION

By Bob Olson

A man's own mind sometimes has a way of telling him more than seven watchmen posted on a high tower.

~ *Wisdom of Ben Sira*

After a year of studying mediums, I heard about a spirit communication technique called "Automatic Writing." This is a process of shutting your conscious mind off to allow your unconscious mind to take over your writing, allowing your spirit-guides to write (communicate) through you. Some think of automatic writing as "channeled" writing where your body (in this case, your hands and fingers) is controlled by spirits. Others think of it more as a means of communication, not allowing spirit to control your body but allowing you to stop the noisy chatter of your conscious thoughts in order to hear what the spirits are saying, or possibly what your higher self has to tell you.

For those of us who will probably never become psychic mediums ourselves, automatic writing is a tool we can use to communicate with spirits on our own. It is a tool that allows people like me and you to communicate with our deceased loved-ones and spirit-guides *without* the need for a psychic medium. When you really think about it, that's pretty cool. Not only will it save us a lot of money on reading fees, it gives us better access to the guidance and ongoing relationships we all have access to with those spirits who love and guide us.

EXPERIMENTING WITH AUTOMATIC WRITING

I decided to give automatic writing a try to see what results I might have. I understood what mediums do to raise their energy and connect with spirit, so I knew the basic process—basically it is meditation, clearing the mind and raising your energy. And I knew it was unlikely that I would ever share the gift that Vicki has as a medium. As a writer, my typing skills were such that my fingers typed words as fast as I could think them. It seemed like an interesting experiment to type my thoughts before I had a chance to think about what I was writing. I wasn't confident that I would be able to do this automatic writing thing, but I knew there was no harm in trying.

I meditated first to get into a relaxed state of mind. I'm not all that great at meditation, but I found it helpful to use headphones and some type of relaxing music to shut off any outside distractions and slow my brainwaves. Unfortunately, I'm one of those people who often falls asleep while meditating. If snoring were a sign of deep meditation, monks and yogis would be at my door asking to learn my secret methods.

Once relaxed, I placed my fingers over my keyboard. I've found that I usually have to ask a question in order to get started; I think that helps amateurs like me. Then I rapidly typed whatever answer popped into my head. Most times I was aware of what I was writing, but didn't have time to edit anything consciously because I was typing so fast. Other times

I felt like my typing was slowing down and my conscious mind might be controlling the process, so I stopped and relaxed my mind again before proceeding.

I did this for a few weeks before I read what I had written. I was a bit shocked at the results. The words really didn't sound like me. First of all, what was written was too wisdom-ish. I'm no guru and I don't write like the great philosophers, yet this stuff was full of wisdom and written with a hint of philosophical flair. Here is an example of one of my automatic writings. Now that you are used to my writing style, you will notice that the words being written are dissimilar to the way I normally write:

You are energy. You are all energy. Energy. Remember yourself as energy and more will begin to make sense. When you remember a past life, when you connect with a person across the country or across the world telepathically, when strange unexplainable coincidences occur that you simply cannot make sense of, this is because you are energy; and until you see yourself as such, you will not be able to make sense of it all.

Energy is all we are. Your temporary human existence is like a ride at Disney World, you are traveling through space inside a body. Consider this body your vehicle. Like your car, you must treat your body well in order to get the most mileage out of it. But do not get too attached to it, it is only temporary. You will have other cars, and thus other bodies.

There are no limitations to your destinations. The only limitations are within your own belief system. You cannot drive to a location that you do not believe exists. You would not even try. If someone told you to drive to Atlantis, you would never leave your driveway. You do not believe it exists, so you would not attempt to get there. The same is true with your destinations in life. If you can think it, you can and will get there. You have heard it said, "You must know where you are going in order to get there." That is related to this concept. It is not really necessary to have a map or route planned out; it is only necessary to have a destination.

"Destinations Unlimited" would be a good title for a book on this teaching. "Think it and it will be" is the lesson. Think of yourself as energy and you can make anything happen. Energy is without limitations. Human form is a sluggish energy, but your mind allows you to make anything happen. Your mind is not sluggish. Your mind is pure energy, and it is faster than light.

Do not let your sluggish human form fool you into thinking you are limited in your power to create change. Remember from where you came, your home. You are energy and you have no limitations. Solid forms are energy, too. Solid forms are those with the lowest movement. Density is the challenge. Density is the challenge of human existence. You must remember that even dense objects are energy, but we as humans often fail to recognize that. By knowing that all is energy, even the densest substances, you will know that everything can be changed.

But change must first happen for humans within their mind. Every change first begins with thought. Thought then sends the signal out into the Universe and it manifests. As a human you cannot know how this manifestation process occurs. So you must trust. But the results will prove to you that is it true, and that will allow you to trust even more the next time. As your trust improves, so will your ability to manifest what you originate in your thoughts. Then it will begin to occur faster.

Belief—knowledge from learning and experience—limits us in human form. You must open your mind to the possibilities of what you want to manifest, not what you think is possible. Do you want to achieve world peace? Then believe it can be done. Trust that it can be done. Do you want to manifest change in form or society or yourself? Then first believe that it is possible, even if you cannot conceive of how that will occur. It is not for you to know how it will occur. It is only for you to imagine. Then focus your thoughts on that outcome. Imagine the details so that your outcome will be able to manifest exactly how you see it in your mind. With the details in your thoughts, the Universal energy will create it as you see it in your mind's eye.

Then simply follow your intuition. If you feel compelled to go somewhere, do it. If you feel compelled to talk to some stranger, do it. If you feel compelled to call someone for help, for advice, for a reason unknown, make that call! Follow what the Universal energy is guiding you to do. It is trying to help you manifest your desires, what is in your mind's eye. By trusting that you are being guided, you will manifest your desired outcome much faster than if you do not assist in the process. Yet, even without your help, if you continue to focus and believe, it will still happen. It may just take a little longer.

Outcomes are achieved in stages. Manifestation does not occur by twinkling your nose, but by progressing through "levels" of manifestation. As these levels progress, pieces of a puzzle are brought together in a way you can not imagine as a human. You can only trust that it is so. As the puzzle is completed, your outcome—your desired thought—will be. This is the power of human thought energy that everyone has but few people know about. Even those who have learned of this great power of manifestation are limited in their ability to use it because of their doubting belief system. You have been one of those people. For years, you studied the power of thought, but never really believed it contained the level of power to create that some people claimed. Now we are telling you that it is true. And there is a reason for you to know this now. There is a purpose for which you need fulfill that only trust in this manifestation process will allow you to achieve. This is the key. It is time for you to open many doors with this key. You must now begin to practice opening doors.

With practice, you will learn the infinite possibilities that exist with this key. And as you gain control of your newfound ability, you will grow in your limitless possibilities, empowering you to make the world a better place, in a way that only you can do. Since we are all so unique, yet so similar, we each have a fingerprint that allows us to touch others in our own way. With this key, it is your time to touch the world in your own way. Open your mind to the possibilities. With this key, what will you do to create change? That is the new question to ask yourself.

WHO IS THAT VOICE IN MY HEAD?

Okay, I don't know about you, but I think that stuff is a little heavy. I prefer a lighter approach. The interesting part is that I was the person who wrote it. The truth is that I'm still slightly skeptical that I have the ability for automatic writing. I'll be the first person to view my automatic writing with a cynical eye. In fact, that's exactly what I did one day while Melissa and I were over Vicki Monroe's house having some friendly conversation and laughs.

"That's great that you've learned to do this," Vicki said about my automatic writing.

"Yeah, but he doesn't fully believe in it," said Melissa.

"What do you mean he doesn't believe in it?" Vicki barked. "He's doing it!" Vicki likes that fact that I still question my new discoveries of the paranormal, but she gets impatient with the *depth* of my skepticism. I always need a ton of evidence before I will begin to accept certain concepts.

Melissa looked at me with one of those, "Well, explain yourself Mr. Skeptical" looks.

"I'll admit that my automatic writing doesn't sound like anything I would write. But I usually know what I'm typing, so it's hard for me to believe that it isn't simply my own thoughts," I told Vicki.

"Well, I know for sure that it's not your own thoughts,

because I know who is coming through—he's right here now," said Vicki.

Melissa and I looked at each other with curious expressions. We knew this was going to be interesting.

"Okay, who is it?" I challenged.

"It's your Uncle Donald," said Vicki.

Just when I think I've got Vicki in a spot where I can prove her wrong, she has to come out with something solid. I actually did have an Uncle Donald, my father's older brother, who had passed a year before my father. I call him Uncle Duck, but mediums often get the formal names before they get nicknames. Still, I wasn't going to let this one pass without a fight. If Uncle Duck was really helping me with my automatic writing, Vicki was going to have to prove it. I needed to know he was really there.

I knew that Vicki had no knowledge about my Uncle Duck. I knew that I never mentioned him to her. And there was something very personal and distinct about Uncle Duck that she could never have known—he had a tattoo on the top of each foot. So I decided to test Vicki to see if she could tell me about these tattoos as evidence that Uncle Duck was really in the room.

"Let's see," I began. "If you can prove to me that Uncle Duck is really here, then I'll believe he is communicating with me through my automatic writing. I'm thinking of something that is very unique about him that would prove to me he's with us now—*if* you can tell me what that is."

"Oh boy," said Melissa to Vicki, "it's not enough that you tell him about his uncle being here, now he has to push it to the limits by testing you."

"In my defense," I protested, "I'm making this easy on her. I'm not asking for a lot. There is one thing Vicki can tell me about Uncle Duck that will prove to me without a doubt that he is here right now. If she gets it, I'll take her word for it that he's the one coming through in my automatic writing. Why else would he be here during this conversation? That's fair, isn't it?"

"Fair enough," said Vicki, "I'll see what he tells me." I gave Melissa one of those, "Nah, nah, na-nah, nah" looks with a shameless smile. Melissa rolled her eyes.

There was a moment of silence while Vicki waited for Uncle Duck to tell her the information I needed. "He's showing me that he loved fishing," said Vicki. That was true. Anyone who knew my uncle also knew he was a serious fishing enthusiast. But that wasn't what I wanted. I wanted the tattoos on his feet! So I told Vicki she was right about the fishing, but that I was looking for something else.

"All right, he tells me that he was in the military," said Vicki. Again, good call. Uncle Duck was on the U.S.S. Enterprise in the Navy during World War II. In fact, he was a war hero who saved the lives of many men during a fire on that aircraft carrier. He also had a lot of military memorabilia from that war around his house. Plus, it was while he was in the Navy that he got the tattoos on his feet. If you knew Uncle Duck, you knew he was in the military; but that wasn't the proof I wanted, so I told Vicki, "Good call, kid, but not what I'm looking for." She took a deep breath, sighed, and looked to Uncle Duck for something more.

"I got it," she said with a smile on her face, "he had a tattoo. That's what you're looking for, isn't it?" said Vicki with certainty that she had got it.

"Not bad, not bad. That is what I wanted. But if you can get that, I need to know *where* the tattoo was on his body," I told Vicki.

Melissa hit me gently as if to say, "Shame on you."

"Hey," I said, "I just want to be sure Uncle Duck is here. If she gets this, I'm convinced."

Vicki sat in silence for a minute. She was sort of lounging on two stools, her body sat on one stool with her feet resting on another like a human bridge. Suddenly, a big smile filled her face and she began wiggling her toes.

"What?" I asked.

"The tattoos where on his feet," she said, knowing she had hit the mark.

"Oh my God, I can't believe you got it," Melissa said.

"Yeah, that's exactly what I was looking for. I can't believe it," I said. I was slightly impressed, yet slightly disappointed that I couldn't stump her. Now it was going to be more difficult to question what was happening with my automatic writing.

I should mention that spirits usually don't like to be tested like this. They want people to learn "trust." Uncle Duck must have really wanted to help me get over my skepticism to put up with me on this one. In fact, several spirits have been very patient with my tests during my research for this book. For this, I am very grateful. My point, however, is that it doesn't hurt to test spirits, but we need to know that some spirits won't play the game if *trust* is the lesson we need to learn.

TRUST & PRACTICE REQUIRED

Automatic writing is an easy form of spirit communication, and many people believe that anyone can do it. Well-known authors like Ruth Montgomery and her mentor, Arthur Ford, have written volumes of books using the gift of automatic writing. Ruth is a lot better at it than me. Nonetheless, I know that half my problem lies within my degree of trust that I'm really doing it. I still continue to have a tiny bit of doubt even after the whole Uncle Duck experience. After all, the only thing Vicki *really* proved was that Uncle Duck was in the room that day. It is not that I think Vicki isn't telling the truth. It's just a gigantic leap for me to connect the dots between Uncle Duck being present that day and the legitimacy of my automatic writing. Still, if my automatic writing really is legit, and it is not just my own mind writing these things, than I have no doubt that it is Uncle Duck coming through. As I mentioned, why else would he have been there during that conversation? He has never spoken at any of my readings.

I have gone through long periods of time without practicing automatic writing, which isn't advised. From what I've learned, the more you do it the better you get at it. For some people, their hands and fingers actually begin moving themselves without any conscious effort—at least that's what I hear. There are people who actually claim they can have a conversation with a person sitting next to them while their hands type something totally unrelated to that conversation, automatically. Others claim to write something *consciously* with one hand while the other hand *subconsciously* writes something different. To me, this type of automatic writing is more like channeled writing, where the spirit basically uses your body to do the writing himself.

Perhaps practice can lead someone from the type of automatic writing that I do (more like mental communication) to this channeled style of automatic writing (where your fingers just move on their own). Personally, however, I believe that the difference between the two styles is related to the degree of ability with which one is born, just as some will play Chopin on the piano and some will struggle with nursery rhymes. I expect I'll always be at the nursery rhyme level with my automatic writing. But never say never; perhaps I'll have better news in my next book.

HOW TO BEGIN

If you want to give automatic writing a try, it's as easy as writing a letter to yourself. Some people recommend saying a prayer of intention and asking God or your spirit guides to surround you in God's light of protection so that only the highest energy beings in God's light are allowed to communicate to you or through you.

Start by getting yourself into a relaxed state of mind. Take several deep breaths; tighten and then loosen all your muscles—from head to toe—one area at a time; and listen to some soothing music, perhaps classical or new age music (best if done with headphones).

When you feel yourself in a relaxed state, put your fingers to the keyboard (if you like to type) or pen to paper (if you prefer this method), and simply write the very first words that come into your mind. As I mentioned, it is usually best for beginners to start with a specific question in mind. Actually write the question onto the paper and then write the first words that pop into your mind as the answer. The trick is to write whatever immediately comes into your head without really thinking about it consciously.

Write as fast as the words come to you so that you don't have time to intellectualize what you're writing. Don't worry about spelling or grammar; this is not going to be graded. Just write the answers to the questions that you asked, and you can read them later (and edit the spelling later, too, if you must).

When you stop writing because nothing more is coming to you, or someone interrupts you, read what you have written. You may be surprised to recognize that the piece you have written will sound nothing like your own writing. Friends and family members may notice this before you do if they are used to reading what you write.

Try to do your automatic writing around the same time every day. Begin doing it for ten or fifteen minutes per session at the most. Soon, both your spirit-guides and your own mind will be trained to anticipate this particular time of day for this communication, and you will find yourself being able to fall right into the relaxed state of mind and into your automatic writing without delay. As you improve, you can continue your automatic writing sessions for longer periods of time.

Do not be discouraged the first few times you try this. It may feel awkward at the beginning, but you will slowly grow accustomed to it. You may also need to learn how to "trust" that what you are writing is actually coming from your spirit-guides and not from your own mind. Chances are, however, the voice you hear will be your own. Don't expect to hear someone else's voice. Imagine that you are writing down a conversation you are having in your head with your higher self. With practice, you will notice that the words you write have a greater wisdom about them than the way you normally speak or write. You will notice that the pattern of speech within the writing is different than your own. And you will eventually learn—as you grow to trust the automatic writing—that the information given to you is beyond any knowledge and experience you previously had before reading it. With practice and consistency, you will gain the wisdom of the spirit-world at your fingertips. Good luck and good writing!

CHAPTER FIFTEEN
INHERITED OR CULTIVATED?
WHAT CHILDREN TEACH US ABOUT
MEDIUMSHIP

By Bob Olson

It is again a strong proof of men knowing most things before birth, that when mere children they grasp innumerable facts with such speed as to show that they are not then taking them in for the first time, but remembering and recalling them.

~ *Cicero*

I n considering the question of whether everyone has the gift of mediumship, I thought it would be interesting to examine both Vicki's childhood as well as that of her children. I wondered if mediums have different childhood experiences than the rest of us, and I hoped my interviews with her children might indicate whether there was a hereditary factor involved in acquiring the gift. My results were quite extraordinary.

SIGNS OF MEDIUMSHIP UNNOTICED

Many mediums recall having childhood experiences that indicated a gift of mediumship as early as age three. Some mediums saw dead relatives in their youth. Others actually carried on a conversation with these spirits. Still, other children seemed to know things psychically that allowed them to predict future events. Despite telling their parents about these events, these childhood signs of a spiritual gift went unnoticed by adults in almost every case.

The few childhood incidents that hinted at Vicki's gift are more vivid in Vicki's memory than in her mother's. This is not surprising since parents of gifted children often fail to notice the signs of the child medium's gift because they write them off as common childhood behavior. This is especially true when the parents do not share in the psychic gifts of their children.

Vicki's mother, Nancy, appears to have some advanced intuitive abilities, but she does not see or hear spirits. In fact, until about fifteen years ago, she didn't give the afterlife much thought. Who would have time for such introspection with five children running around (or four children up until the time Vicki was eight, when her sister, Amy, was born)? Nancy admits, "When you have four children, with so much happening, you miss some stuff. I'm sure there were signs of Vicki's gift when she was younger, but I don't remember them. I don't say this with guilt; I'm just saying there must have been some signs that I probably just thought of as cute and funny."

MONK OR HUNK?

Nancy did recall a couple happenings that she considered odd. "There was one incident when Vicki was ten or eleven. We were looking at old papers that I had stored, and we came across the children's baptism cards. Vicki said to me, 'I remember the man who baptized me...' then Vicki described this small elderly man in a brown Friar Tuck-like robe with a rope around his waist. She said he had a long beard, was stocky and had sandals on his feet." Nancy laughed softly as she continued, "I, too, was at the baptism, and that's not the same man I saw. The minister who baptized all four of my children at that ceremony, including Vicki, was over six-feet tall, blonde, clean-shaven, and a physically fit young guy in his mid-thirties wearing a black robe. I remembered him clearly because he was a pretty darn good-looking guy," she giggled.

"Vicki was only about four years old at the baptism, so when she told me this story at age ten, I just thought she was being cute. The man she described was so far off from the truth..." Nancy trailed off, her thoughts floating off in the distance. "I thought she was just being a kid," she finished.

Vicki recalls the baptism like it was only yesterday. This isn't surprising since memories of spiritual occurrences are usually more vivid than memories of normal everyday events. Whether it be childhood incidents where monks appear instead of ministers, "visitation dreams" where deceased loved-ones come to say hello while we are sleeping, or near-death experiences where people die, cross-over into the afterlife and then return back to life, the distinct memories of these experiences seem to never fade with time. Vicki has described the baptism story to me a multitude of times, but she never sways in her articulate recall. Here is how she once described it to me:

As a four-year-old standing at the alter to be baptized, and after my two brothers and one sister had taken their turn, I stood up, raised my head, and to my surprise an old, matronly looking monk with several monks on both sides of him, stood staring down at me. He smiled and held my hand in his. I hesitated slightly, but it felt right somehow so I wasn't scared. The monk spoke softly to me, telling me that the scene was mine alone to behold, although I didn't understand what he was talking about at the time.

He then reached into a large stone bowl of water, and with his thumb he pressed against my forehead as he repeated the word 'Sight' several times over. I felt such a sense of calm at the pressure of his hand on my forehead that I almost fell asleep standing up. I remember stumbling backward a bit, and when I reached out to get my balance, the hand that reached out to me belonged to a 35-year-old blonde minister rather than the monk. The monk who had, for lack of a better word, 'christened' me, was now gone, including the monks who surrounded him.

It wasn't until weeks later that I told my mother about the old monk. I don't think she had any idea what I was telling her. And it wasn't until I was ten that he visited me again.

SCARLET FEVER

Following this unusual baptismal event, Vicki continued to be an ordinary young girl for the next six years. It wasn't until the age of ten that, as she mentioned above, another exhilarative episode took place. This time, a bout with scarlet fever initiated another visit from her bearded-monk friend. Here's how Vicki described it to me:

As I have mentioned previously, it wasn't until the age of 10, as a fourth grader, that I saw the monk again. This time, however, the circumstances were different. I was diagnosed with scarlet fever. For ten days I was isolated from my family. The words I overheard from adults talking were, 'possible blindness,' 'brain damage,' and several other possible consequences that echoed through the hallway. I noticed a lot of relatives were now visiting who rarely came to visit. I concluded that I must be dying.

One night, after a long day with a high fever, I began to feel sorry for myself. I remember wondering if I would ever feel well again, that maybe I really was going to die. It was then that the monk with the long beard—the same monk from my baptism—appeared at the foot of my bed. He was standing, actually more like hovering, there looking at me. I couldn't see his feet; his hands were wrapped into his cloak; and his face was partially hidden by his hood.

I can't say that I didn't feel some fear this time; I was definitely afraid. As he moved closer and leaned over me, I realized that I couldn't move, like I was paralyzed. I wanted to scream, but I couldn't do that either. Then he sort of sighed and it felt like his breath touched me. It actually felt like his breath cooled my fever. I just laid there in my bed unable to move.

The monk then reached out his hand and touched my forehead like he did at the baptism. Again, he whispered, "Sight," before smiling at me and then floating away. Then he just disappeared. I remember sitting up and feeling like my fever was gone. Then I just went to sleep.

The next morning when I got up, I ran into the kitchen where my mother was making me some tea. I remember asking her if I could have something good instead of tea because I was starving. She just stared at me in disbelief. I felt great and was running around like normal. It wasn't until later that evening when I sat down to dinner with my family that I told them about the monk returning. Nobody said anything, but my mother looked at me and squeezed my hand. I felt like she believed me, this time.

Wouldn't that be a nice story if Vicki's mother, Nancy, finally recognized that her daughter's "fairytales" were real? But this is reality, folks. Nancy told me that she remembers Vicki telling her about the monk after the scarlet fever mysteriously disappeared, but that squeeze on the hand had "patronize" written all over it. I can just imagine the wink Nancy must have given her husband, Charlie, as she responded to little Vicki, "Sure, honey, I'm sure he *is* the same man you saw at your baptism." And then I'll bet she leaned over and whispered to Charlie, "Wow, that was *some* fever…"

I'm kidding, of course. But Nancy did admit to me, "I really didn't think much about it. I assumed it was either the fever or she was just being a kid." If you are wondering, "How could Nancy not pay attention to that?" The answer is simple: We all know, even if we don't have children, that parents listen to thousands of stories every week from their children. Imagine Nancy with five little rascals running around. It is hard enough paying attention to their basic needs; are most parents supposed to be on the lookout for mystical encounters as well? Maybe if your Dana Sculley or Fox Mulder from *The X-Files*, but the Nancy Chadbournes often use up all their energy just trying to handle life on *this* side of the ethereal barrier.

CAN CHILDREN SEE DEAD PEOPLE?

It is important to note that most children are much more "in tune" with their psychic abilities than adults, probably because they haven't yet been *trained* to trust and rely on their other five senses more than their sixth sense. Just the fact that children have not been away from the spirit world long may also be a factor for their increased awareness.

It is not uncommon for children to see and talk with their spirit-guides or the spirits of deceased relatives (even if they aren't guides). Yet, many parents write this off as their child having an "imaginary friend." I heard of one mother who recently asked her son who he was talking to all the time. When he named, and accurately described, his grandfather, the mother questioned further. Within fifteen minutes, her son told her several details about his grandfather. The interesting part was that the boy's grandfather had died before he was born. Even more amazing, the parents had never talked about the grandfather in front of the boy because they thought he was too young to understand the concept of death. I guess the boy had a more discerning understanding of the afterlife than his parents realized.

Children may also retain memories of their past lives. I have a friend whose daughter often makes off-the-cuff remarks like, "No Mommy, Sandy's not your sister, she's *my* daughter," and "Mommy, Nana is *my* mommy, not yours." This three-year-old has been making these comments ever since she could talk, usually correcting her mother for stating these relationships erroneously. The mother always considered the comments "child's talk" until I began telling her of similar stories. It was after my narration of these stories that she confessed her own daughter's account. Today, she no longer debates these associations with her daughter, accepting that they are *both* correct.

So what happens when you grow up with a mother who understands matters of the spirit and isn't afraid of them? You end up with children like those of Vicki and Bret Monroe: Ryan, Josh, Adam and Amelia. Over the last four years, I've had the privileged opportunity to know them and interview them on this subject. What they have to say about spiritual matters speaks volumes.

I initially interviewed Ryan and Josh, Vicki's eldest sons, only ten months after first meeting Vicki. At the ages of fifteen and fourteen, respectively, these boys were still willing to talk openly about their spiritual experiences. I interviewed Adam (at age thirteen) and Amelia (at age eleven) a couple years later. At these ages, it is difficult getting much more than "yes" or "no" answers. I suspect it would have been more difficult if I interviewed them with their older brothers two years prior. Still, like their older brothers, Adam and Amelia had no hesitation talking about their experiences with spirit, which were quite insightful. I believe most children their age wouldn't *understand* half my questions, never mind give me insightful answers.

VISITATION DREAMS, SPIRIT SIGHTINGS & PREMONITIONS

Ryan told me about visitation dreams where he has been visited by his grandfather and his Aunt Heather (Vicki's younger sister who died in an auto accident). Like most visitation dreams, Ryan says these dreams are very clear and in color. "After I dream about them, I feel like I just saw them so they aren't really gone," said Ryan. "I feel like they are visiting me in my dream," he added, "and it makes me feel good to know they are around."

His brother, Josh, has seen his grandfather the same way Vicki sees spirits. "Our Papa is around. I've seen him. Sometimes he just walks by and, a second later, he disappears." I asked Josh if he was scared when he saw his grandfather. "No, it was comforting. Knowing he is still here is very comforting," Josh told me.

Josh said he sees his grandfather two or three times a year. So I asked Josh about the first time he ever saw him.

"In the old house before this one, we had a desk in my room. I woke up to go to the bathroom and Papa was just sitting on the small desk. Neither of us said anything. He was wearing a cloak with sandals and his skin was a blue color; I don't know why. I waved to him as I walked to the bathroom and he waved back. It was as if I see him all the time. I guess I expected he would still be there when I got back. When I returned, he was gone. It wasn't a dream; it was definitely real, but at first I wondered if I was dreaming. Then I realized I was awake and I was happy to have seen him," said Josh.

Adam shares the family gift as well. Vicki expects that if any of her children grow up to use their gift professionally, it is likely to be Adam.

"I saw a woman once," said Adam, referring to a spirit he had seen. "She was wearing white and was just sitting on the couch. It was the middle of the day, so I wasn't dreaming. It was sort of scary, but sort of not because I knew from Mom that she wasn't going to hurt me. I just saw her for a few seconds and then she was gone," said Adam.

"Another time, I was on the bus when I looked out the window and saw some people riding like a carriage kind of thing with horses pulling it. It looked like they were from a different time because of the clothes they were wearing. It looked different than if it were real people, but I couldn't see through them like you might expect to see through spirits. But then I asked my friends on the bus if they saw them and they said they didn't see anything. So I figured they were ghosts or something," explained Adam.

Adam has also had what I would conclude to be visitation dreams, but he doesn't recognize the people he sees. "It's not anybody I know," said Adam. "I just see their heads and faces. I see them real quick. It's like they smile and then I wake up. I don't think they have a message for me, not that I can remember," he added.

Those aren't the only kinds of dreams Adam has experienced. He also has premonition dreams now and then. "I often have dreams where I dream something and then it happens in real life," said Adam. I learned that this is something the other children regularly experience as well.

Adam's older brother, Ryan, told me the same thing in my interview with him about two years earlier.

"Sometimes I dream of something and the next day I find myself doing that exact thing, in the exact same situation," Ryan told me. Amelia, the youngest of the siblings, has had similar dreams.

"Sometimes I'll have a dream and then it will happen the next day. Or in a week or so, I'll remember that I saw those same people before in my dream," Amelia told me.

While it is not uncommon that people experience this sort of phenomena, Vicki's children seem to experience it more often than most. They don't describe it as feeling like déjà vu, but rather a premonition of what is about to take place. Déjà vu is more of a "feeling" that something has already taken place, a feeling of familiarity with a person, place or event. What Adam, Amelia and Ryan have described is not just a feeling, but a vivid memory of a dream that was more like a snapshot of the future than a indescribable sensation.

Are these kids just better able to remember their dreams, as if they have an enhanced recall of their dreams, while most of us only experience that thing called déjà vu? Or are many children having these same experiences but nobody is interviewing them about them or listening when they speak about them? Or finally, are Vicki's children simply more open to these experiences because their mother has taught them not to push them away and feel foolish or ashamed to have them and talk about them? Perhaps the fact that Vicki talks to her children about such phenomena, and that they acknowledge these events in their conversations with her, allows them to both remember them more and allow them to occur without pushing them away.

Amelia has also seen spirits like her mother. "I had just gone to bed for the night once when I saw my Aunt Heather standing near my doorway. She was very clear and all white. She didn't say anything to me, but it made me feel good to see her. It made me feel happy to know that she is still here," Amelia explained.

Amelia has seen other spirits as well. "Every once in awhile I see quick glimpses of people walking by my bedroom door. These are just people who are in the house though; I don't know who they are. It's sort of scary because they walk by real quick and then they are gone. A couple times I've got up and looked in the hall, but nobody was there. Usually I don't even look. Sometimes, if I have to go to the bathroom, I don't even go because I'm scared to walk out of my room," she said laughing.

After hours of interviewing Vicki's children, and now having known them since 1999, I can tell you that Ryan, Josh, Adam and Amelia are some of the most level-headed down-to-earth kids you could ever meet. They achieve high grades in school, are active in several extra-curricular activities, and are some of the most polite and well-mannered kids I've had the pleasure to know. So, in case you were wondering what effects it might have on children to know that spirits exist and watch over us, these are four healthy examples to indicate positive results from such a childhood knowing.

Perhaps we should be asking ourselves what the implications are for *not* helping our children with their spiritual development. I'm not referring to religion, necessarily, as most people do not hesitate to expose their children to religious beliefs. Instead, I am referring to the attention adults give to the spiritually related experiences their children are having, regardless of their religious affiliation or beliefs.

IMAGINARY FRIENDS OR SPIRIT GUIDES?

My wife, Melissa, used to have an imaginary friend named Sally while growing up. At least that is what adults taught her to believe—that Sally was imaginary. It wasn't until we had begun learning that children often see and communicate with spirits that Melissa realized her friend, Sally, may not have been imaginary at all. It may have been that Sally was a spirit-guide, or someone from the spirit world with whom Melissa had shared a past life. I don't know why some children have relationships with spirits in their younger years, but Melissa's story is not uncommon.

If your child is having conversations with someone invisible to your eyes, don't assume there isn't really someone there. I don't mean to imply that children do not make up people in their imaginations; I'm sure that many do. But my research has indicated that many children, like the childhood version of Vicki Monroe, have seen or communicated with people not of this world. Vicki was taught by adults that such behavior wasn't acceptable. We can only speculate how things might have been different had her parents been more open to the possibility that her claims were not just imaginary, childhood nonsense or "kids being kids," but were real experiences.

Still, parents cannot be held to blame for the reactions of other adults when it comes to these matters. Teachers, neighbors, aunts and uncles will all have an affect on a child when they react to his or her claims of spirit contact. Children are impressionable. This is how we learn what is acceptable behavior in society. If enough adults tell a child that he couldn't have really talked to Aunt Betty at the funeral home because she was laying dead in the casket, eventually that child will learn to accept this as truth. Resultantly, these impressionable children may begin pushing away their unacceptable visions or communications with spirits because they don't want to be laughed at or seen as a freak anymore.

On the other hand, Vicki's children sway me to believe that even one open-minded parent can have a positive effect on a child that can offset the limiting beliefs projected by other adults. When asked if they tell other people about what their mother does for a living, all four of Vicki's children admitted that they are selective with whom they share this information. Every one of them told me, in slightly different words, that "some people are not ready to believe."

The good news is that society is undoubtedly shifting in our spiritual consciousness. Today I have friends who—once rock-solid skeptics—now watch John Edward's television show, *Crossing Over With John Edward*, ritually. Who would have guessed? Plus, last year there were probably more bestselling books on the subject of mediumship than on any other single subject. What does it mean? It means that people's minds are opening to the possibilities. And with this societal shift comes a change in attitude that will be passed down to our children, if only subconsciously. For this reason, I don't fret about the limiting beliefs that adults spread to the next generation. I simply trust in the process. I trust that everything is working just the way it should.

CHAPTER SIXTEEN
A MEDITATION FOR SPIRIT
COMMUNICATION

By Vicki Monroe

Grant me the ability to be alone; may it be my way every day to go outdoors among the trees and grasses, among all growing things, and there may I be alone, to talk with the one that I belong to.

~ Prayer of Rabbi Nachman of Bratzlav

About a year ago, a major event promoter in Puerto Rico discovered OfSpirit.com on the Internet and read Bob's article about his first reading with me. She then contacted me about doing an event there. She had one stipulation: in addition to doing my regular medium demonstration, I also had to do a two-hour workshop. She said this is what she required of all her guests, including Dr. Wayne Dyer and Deepak Chopra, M.D. So I said, "Sure, how hard can it be?" Then, as usual, I panicked after hanging up the phone, not knowing what kind of workshop I could offer.

After some serious contemplation, and talking to numerous people who regularly give workshops, I decided to simply give a guided meditation. I wanted to teach people the same meditation I do myself in order to meet with my personal spirit-guides and loved ones in spirit.

TEARS & SHOCK IN PUERTO RICO

This workshop was possibly the most amazing experience of my career. I witnessed hundreds of people connect with their deceased loved ones or spirit-guides without the assistance of a medium. They each had their own private connection with spirit. All I did was guide their visualization.

As I stood on stage directing the movie in their minds, I began to see tears flowing down people's faces. Some audience members were smiling. Some were flat out sobbing. I'd be lying if I didn't admit that I was surprised. No, shocked was more my state of mind. But what a lovely surprise it was. By the time the workshop was over, I was crying from the sheer beauty of what I had just witnessed.

The people of Puerto Rico are some of the most spiritual people I have ever had in an audience. They are also full of gratitude and kindness. The people at this event smothered me with gifts of which I did not feel deserving, but accepted as a loving exchange of energy: a piece of stained glass from a church, a handkerchief, a flower... their gifts were both thoughtful and meaningful. I was overwhelmed with love and gratitude from these people, making my experience there more powerful than I could ever have imagined.

Since this meditation worked so well for the people at this event, I have now repeated it with audiences at almost all my events. It has been so successful for people that I decided to share it with you in this section on discovering your own gift of mediumship. I recommend that you either do this with a friend, taking turns reading it to one another, or read it into a tape recorder and play it back for yourself. If you use the tape recorder approach, be sure to speak softly and slowly. And at the appropriate moments, be sure to leave some silent time for your communication with your loved one in spirit or your spirit-guide.

THE MEDITATION

Welcome to this visual meditation. I recommend that you put some soothing music on quietly in the background, preferably music without lyrics so they do not distract you. During this time, I'd like you to lie down on a bed, sofa or on the floor, whatever is comfortable for you. You may want to put cushions under your feet. Every time you meditate or link with spirit, it is recommended that you set an intention to link only with the higher energies of the spirit world by simply saying, "May I connect only with the higher energies that exist in the light and love of God." Now relax and start breathing.

Take three deep breaths at first. Then begin breathing naturally and normally, in through your nose and out through your mouth. Don't over extend your abdomen. Just breath naturally and normally. Listen to the music and it's soothing and angelic sound. Imagine that the music comes from heaven's angels who are singing just for you, and the love that you hear in their voices is for you and you alone. These voices are guiding you to a special place, to a place that is just for you.

I want you to breath and relax every muscle in your body, and with every exhale a different part of your body relaxes until you are almost floating. As you're floating, you rise up, you go out the window or door and you are heading towards a gate. You see this gate and as you slowly touch the ground, you feel the warmth of the sun, not blistering hot, not too cool, but just a perfect warmth that surrounds you. The angels are singing and this wonderful warm, loving light of the sun makes you feel comfortable and safe.

You are on a journey to meet with a loved one in spirit or your spirit-guide. You can now hear their voice in the distance surrounded by the angels' music. They are calling you toward the gate. Listen to them call you. Listen to the angels singing for you. Listen to the love and the sound of the music they play for you. So much love exists behind this gate. This is your very special place. Imagine the doorway to this gate, however you choose to imagine it. Is it made of wrought iron? Is it ornate, or simple and plain? This is your gate. You get to choose.

The angels are calling you to open the gate. They sing to you and only you. Only you can enter this gate unless you wish to invite someone else along. Feel the texture of the gate. Feel its strength. As you look at it, a soft subtle breeze blows on your skin. You still feel the warmth of the sun all around you. Now you can feel the angels' love pouring down upon you. You stand in front of the gate prepared for your journey.

See the latch on your gate. Touch it. Feel its warmth from baking in the warm sun. You instantly feel a white light rush through your body as you lift the latch and open the gate. As you step through the gate, the grass on your feet is soft and warm. With the sun still shining, the music is drawing you in. The angels are welcoming you to a magical land.

In front of you is a pathway amidst a grand forest. Stand for a moment looking down this pathway that will lead you to your special place. As you begin walking down this pathway, the birds sing louder. Hear the rustle of the trees, perhaps they are pines and maples. Hear the whistle of the wind. Feel it soft upon your skin. Stop for a minute. Enjoy the moment. Spread your arms out. Close your eyes. Feel as if every worry and every trouble has been left behind you now. You are free. You begin to float with the air, barely touching the pine needle path within this immense forest. You are led by the voices of angels and the calling of your loved one in spirit or your spirit-guide.

You hear water. There is a brook to the right of your wooded path. You look above and see the sun's rays shining through the trees. In the distance you see a deer gracefully crossing your path. The deer looks toward you. Its eyes lock with yours and you are one with it. You are one with everything. Your body tingles with anticipation. You hear the subtle sound of music and the calling of your name, always remembering that this is your place and no one else can go here but you. You are safe and comfortable.

Keep walking along your path. Hear the bubbling brook to your right. Close your eyes and smell the green moss on the rocks. Smell the clear, clean water as it bubbles over the rocks and logs. These are the experiences of nature. Hear the trees creaking and the birds performing their symphony. They are welcoming you home. You realize this place feels familiar. You get a chill up your spine.

Stop for a moment by the bubbling brook underneath the shade of the big pine tree. You see the pine needles covering the path and you can almost taste the scent of the forest. Kneel down feeling the cool earth beneath your knees. Reach to pick up a handful of pine needles, feeling their texture between your fingers as you let them slowly drop to the ground. Gently lean forward to put your hands in the cool water of the flowing brook. Feel the sensation of the water as it runs over your hands. Cup your hands full of water and lift it to your lips, quenching your thirst. Sit for a moment and breath in the moist air above the water, feeling the coolness of it, smelling the scent of it and listening to it trickling over the rocks. Just fill your senses and breathe. Taking one last deep breath by the brook, stand again and begin to walk away back down your path.

Just ahead, you see a small hill, which fills you with excitement. You rush towards it, exhilarated, almost flying; your feet and body are so light. As you ascend the hill, you look out to fill your eyes with brilliant colors. It is a vast valley of fragrant wild flowers. Every scent that you can imagine is wafting through the air... gardenias, roses, jasmine... it all flows through your senses. It is a magical place.

You see bumblebees and humming birds busily going about their work. There is such beauty here and you are a part of this beauty. Stare out over the valley. Walk down the hill feeling the flowers and their softness, almost as if they are kissing your knees and caressing your legs. You realize that the love that connects every living thing is touching you because you are a part of it. All things that live, love. And all things that die, return, just as you do. You are on a spiritual journey.

Continue now to walk, feeling the flowers around you. In the distance, you start to hear a different sound. You soon figure out that what you are hearing is the ocean. You begin to taste the sea air, which is blowing softly across your face and through your hair. You hear seagulls and the loving voice of a loved one in spirit or your spirit-guide inviting you to come forward to the beach, to this beautiful sacred place. As you step over a rise, you see that the sun is just beginning to set in the sky above the ocean. You feel your feet in the soft, pure, crystal-white sand. The setting sun is scarlet and purple reflecting on the water that looks like glass. Dolphins are dancing together in the distance, never making a ripple in the water.

As you approach the shoreline, you feel the salt water on your feet. The water is calm, but there is a slight wake, rhythmically washing your skin as the water moves up and down your ankles. With each tiny wave, chills run through your body.

It is time to invite the loved one in spirit or your spirit-guide to join you. You look down the beach and see them in the distance. Walk towards them. They are here for you. You now know that they never left you. Keep walking towards them. They are getting closer. You can now see their expression and the radiance of their face smiling back at you. You are filled with the most profound love, greater than you have ever felt before. You reach out to one another. Your fingers touch. Your hands join. You hug one another, feeling the essence of their unconditional love flowing through every cell of your body. They never left you. They never *will* leave you. This love is forever.

Walk towards the ocean with your loved one, holding each other as you go, feeling every memory, every wonderful moment you have ever had together. There is no sadness here, only joy. Tell your loved one or spirit guide what you wish to say to them. This is the moment to ask them any questions you have, to give or request forgiveness, or to ask for guidance. Take however much time you need. Savor the moment.

It is now time for you to leave. Say your goodbyes, knowing that your loved one or spirit guide is always with you and that you can return to this place at any time. Look over the calm ocean one more time, as the sun slowly sets behind the horizon. You are walking away from the sea now, returning toward the rise where your path begins. Look back and wave to your loved one. You turn back toward the forest, feeling the breeze of the meadow and smelling the scent of the flowers. You descend down the hill, walking through the flowers once again, feeling the love and magic of this place. In the distance you see the deer cross the path. You hear the birds welcoming you back into the forest. You hear the brook approaching. You feel the flowers kissing your legs goodbye, and you start to feel the softness of the pine needles on your feet. The brook is becoming a little louder, and the angels are singing. This isn't goodbye; it is until we meet again. You feel happy. You feel more alive than you have ever felt before. Comfort fills your entire body as you walk, knowing that you can feel this way whenever you return to this place. Just by breathing this way, you can be here again.

You see the clearing and in the far distance you see the gate. Feeling no sadness, only a deep feeling of love, safety and comfort, all your worries and fears have dissipated. Walk closer to the gate, looking one last time behind you, taking another deep breath and feeling all the love that exists in the world. You smile, knowing that those that you love, both living and passed, can join you in this place if you allow it to be so.

Touch the warmth of the gate's latch, lifting it and opening the gate door. Take a deep breath and walk through the gate. Closing the gate behind you, stop for moment to be grateful for the experience you just had. Put your arms out to your sides, once again feeling the breeze and the last rays of the setting sun. The path is behind you. Closing your eyes and breathing, you are floating again. The wind has picked you up like a feather. You are floating on the wind back to your home. The window or door is open for you and you float through it, feeling more at peace than you have ever felt. All worries, discomforts and fears are gone. Only love, passion and peace exist within you. You are landing on your bed, sofa or floor softly and gently, breathing deeply as you awake. Open your eyes and feel the peace. Always remember that you can return to this place whenever you wish.

PART VI
Coming Full Circle

CHAPTER SEVENTEEN
CONNECTED BY AN ETHERIAL THREAD

By Vicki Monroe

I now understand that my welfare is only possible if I acknowledge my unity with all people of the world without exception.

~ Leo Tolstoy

There was a period of about a year when Bob and I were so busy doing our own things that we rarely saw one another anymore. Interestingly, however, as Bob and I were learning and growing on our own separate journeys, our lives were always connected in one way or another. It was as if the Universe was going out of its way to keep us in each other's life.

It makes sense, of course, that Bob's work teaching the public about psychic mediumship would continue to affect me, especially since thousands of people each week were reading about me on his website, OfSpirit.com. He promoted my events there, published a profile on me and even published the article he had written about his first reading with me on that site. Yet, aside from all this, there was an even more significant thread that connected us, and this thread was made apparent when people mysteriously began contacting Bob in order to connect with me.

THE RADIO SYNDICATION EXECUTIVE

One such request came from a radio syndication executive during this time when Bob and I hadn't been in contact in a while. Bob received this email:

Hi there Mr. Olson,

I am in need of some assistance... I am in search of a psychic for a new syndicated radio program. My problem is that I have no idea what makes a good psychic. So as I surf the net in search of one I am becoming exhausted by the sheer number of psychics on the internet. I came across your site OfSpirit and was quite impressed that you actually gave out some useful info without asking for money.

So I'm basically looking for a name or two of a unknown psychic that I can help bring to the world, they can be American, Canadian or from any part of the world as long as their English is understandable. Any ideas would be greatly appreciated.

Bob emailed this man the links to all the articles he had written on psychic mediums. After reading Bob's article about his first reading with me, the radio producer phoned Bob to ask his opinion on whether I would be comfortable doing a radio show. By now, I shouldn't have to tell you how *that* conversation went. Thus, Bob set up a meeting between me and the producer. Nevertheless, after several meetings, nothing ever became of the show but it was the first in a series of encounters that kept Bob and I connected. Alone, this incident would not have been significant. But in light of the incidents that followed, a pattern became evident.

THE DOCUMENTARY FILMMAKER

The same month, a documentary filmmaker contacted Bob. The filmmaker's mother had read Bob's article about his first reading in a local holistic magazine. She then had a reading with me and her experience enticed her son—the filmmaker—to send Bob this email:

Dear Mr. Olson,

...You have recently been in correspondence with my mother Natalia—who just had a very impacting reading with Vicki Monroe. A few months ago, I read your article on Ms. Monroe and was absolutely captivated by your story. My mother's visit only intensified and confirmed my personal belief in your story and the power of what lies beyond the physical realm.

The reason for my writing you is because of my love for making films. I am a documentary filmmaker, and having done a recent award-winning portrait on the life of my grandmother... I am fascinated by characters and their abilities to survive life's obstacles only to arrive at a spiritual resolution... I do not know where to begin in contemplating the many levels that may exist for Ms. Monroe. From gift to burden, this form of communication is, to say the least, astonishing. In pursuing such a subject (which I have never done)...I would only hope to capture her story and show her as the human being she is... with an extraordinary ability.

So with this email, I am wondering if you would be interested in such a project.

I could go on about my thoughts for this, but I should allow you to answer first. Do not hesitate to question me or check my background. Thank you for your time.

What was strange about this was that the filmmaker contacted Bob instead of me. Bob wasn't sure why he did this. After all, my contact information was easier to obtain than his. Being a former private investigator who once investigated murder cases and an author who, strangely enough, has had a few readers trying to locate his house, Bob is somewhat cautious when it comes to giving out his contact info. Plus, the filmmaker's own mother had visited me for a reading. Surely, she had my contact information. But since the filmmaker had contacted him, and since Bob knew that if he told him to contact me directly that I would be calling Bob anyway to ask his opinion, he discussed the proposed project with him and got a feel for his intent and character prior to setting up a meeting with me.

Bob liked what the filmmaker had to say, but told him that the best he could do was to set up a phone call with me. After several meetings, the filmmaker and I came to an agreement and filming began. The project began over a year ago and is still in progress as I write this.

THE FILM PRODUCER

The next strange incident followed within a couple weeks of the documentary filmmaker's email. This time, a film producer emailed Bob with an idea to create a television show on spirit communication using me as the medium host. Here is that email:

Dear Mr. Olson,

I recently read the article in the Maine Sunday Telegram about Vicki Monroe with great fascination. As a producer/director living in the Portland area I couldn't help think that Ms. Monroe could potentially command a wide national audience with a television program. Because you have worked with her in different mediums I am writing to you to introduce myself and to share a few of my thoughts about why television might be a good fit for Ms. Monroe.

When talking about audience appeal, I believe it's not only Ms. Monroe's ability to make you a believer, but also to create emotion in her audiences—to reduce someone to joyful tears one moment and then to get them to laugh in the next. This is sincere and cathartic entertainment. Oprah has been doing this for years.. It's also Ms. Monroe's ability to create hope for people. In her words from the article, "I hope people take away a sense of peace, that they start recognizing that life is eternal. If you understand that, then death may be a little easier to bear." In Ms. Monroe's lectures and readings, her audiences

can vicariously experience those swings of emotion, become be.
and find hope. Because people want so badly to believe in something
to nurture their hope—there is great demand out there.

Ms. Monroe is telegenic and seems to have the ability to keep
people in the moment. After reading the article, I immediately had a
vision for a television show. Television as you know can be produced
where the talent lives. I think that one of her local "Lessons In The
Light"
lectures could serve well as a pilot. I have a full crew that could
shoot it. I would be glad to create a show treatment for you and Ms.
Monroe to read, but I would like to talk with you further about
whether a television show is within the realm of possibility or not.
Thank you.

Again, Bob found it strange that the film producer emailed him, but he talked with the guy and had him mail the treatment he wrote that described the show's format. Bob liked him and thought the treatment was well thought out and written. Bob then forwarded the treatment to me and I loved its concept so much that I called the film producer immediately. After numerous meetings, telephone calls, creation and preparation, the idea blossomed into a demo tape featuring one show. Serendipitously, before we even had time to begin contacting television networks to present the demo, the local UPN/WB executives called me to discuss doing a show on their network. We negotiated the contract and before we had time to realize what was happening, a four-show television series was being aired.

THE MUSIC TV NETWORK PRODUCER

Next, Bob received a call from a producer of a major music TV network. They were considering an ongoing segment where a psychic medium, or several psychic mediums, gave readings where rock stars came through giving messages to their fans. Bob explained to the producer that mediumship doesn't work in this way; that is, a medium can't conjure up anyone they please. He explained that it might work if a deceased rock star's family was at the reading, but the producer wanted only fans to be there. In spite of Bob's advice, the producer wanted to give it a try to see for himself. Having read about me on OfSpirit.com, he asked Bob to set up a reading with me. Of course, Bob was correct, I can't just conjure anyone I please, so I couldn't give the producer what he wanted. The last I knew, the producer was going to try finding a medium who could give him what he wanted. But like trying to fit a square peg into a round hole, I don't expect he will find what he's seeking, at least not from a legitimate medium.

THE TV PILOT PRODUCER

Finally, Bob was contacted by a producer in Los Angeles who was making a TV pilot for a show on mediums. This time, Bob just gave her my phone number and told her to call me. He was beginning to realize that this might never end. He didn't mind screening people for me as a friend, but this was occurring so often that he felt more like my manager than my friend. He joked that he was starting to answer his phone, "Vicki Monroe's office, can I help you?"

I ended up passing on the pilot. I didn't like the intent behind the show—it treated mediumship like a sideshow—so I passed on it despite the temptation of working with some big names in television.

NEW BEGINNINGS, SUSPICIOUS ENDINGS

By this time, Bob and I were seeing each other much more often. Bob and Melissa had begun organizing an event where five psychic mediums would do live demonstrations for five hours on stage. They were the first in this country that I know of to offer such a unique event with mediums, although it is exciting to now see similar events being offered by promoters, including the famed John Edward, in other parts of the country. Since I was one of the five mediums to demonstrate, and since I was helping to promote the event on my weekly radio show, Bob and I were in contact more often than ever. All this contact had us talking by phone at least once a week. Plus, Bob, Melissa, Bret and I began going out to dinner regularly to mix some much-needed non-medium-related fun into the relationship. Once all this took place, people suspiciously stopped trying to contact me through Bob.

As of today, about a year since the first email came in, Bob hasn't received a single email or phone call on my behalf, despite the fact that much of the media who call me for interviews do so because they first read about me on Bob's websites, OfSpirit.com and BestPsychicMediums.com. One might expect that he would continue to get at least *some* of these calls or emails, but he doesn't.

To me, this is just another indication that the radio producer, documentary filmmaker, film producer, music TV network producer and television pilot producer were contacting Bob simply due to some universal effort to keep us connected. Why? Who knows? I can only guess that it was to finish what we had started in January 1994—this book.

CHAPTER EIGHTEEN
FALSE PROMISES, HARD LESSONS &
INCREASED WISDOM

By Vicki Monroe

What is needed is a realization that power without love is reckless and abusive, and love without power is sentimental and anemic.

~ *Martin Luther King, Jr.*

After that first radio interview with Bob and Melissa on The John Alexandrov Show, that moment when I first caught the bug to spread my message to the masses, I now realize how ill prepared I was for the task. I knew nothing about television producers, documentary filmmakers and the like. I grew up in a small town in Southern Maine and I didn't know anyone who was experienced with this stuff. Hence, I was an open target for anyone who came my way claiming they could help me fulfill my mission.

FALSE PROMISES

Bret and Bob kept telling me that people would come out of the woodwork to make me promises, especially with all the publicity I was getting from my weekly radio show, newspapers, magazines and local TV news stations. Yet they said this like it was a *bad* thing. I didn't want to believe it.

I believed in fate. I believed that people were inherently good. And thus far in my journey as a spirit messenger, my life had been magical. So when people arrived in my life promising to help me, I guess I was easy prey; that is, my choices probably could have been better. No, not *probably*, my choices definitely could have been better, because in hindsight I now recognize that my intuition was trying to guide me. I just wasn't listening.

When the radio syndication executive contacted me (after first emailing Bob), he made lots of promises. He said the show he was creating was to be aired across the nation. He made comparisons to shows with Dr. Laura, Rush Limbaugh and Howie Carr. Because he was so forthcoming and enthusiastic, I put everything on hold, just as he asked. He told me that my schedule would quickly become filled, so I needed to weed out some of my events. After giving him and other people in his office personal readings, sending him my press packet with videos of shows I had done, and having several long phone meetings with him, he spoke to me like he was unduly impressed and everything was underway—as if we only needed to sew up a few details.

Being inexperienced in this area, I took what he said literally and got excited. Bob kept repeating, "Don't get excited until it actually happens, Vicki. This man's world is high on promises and low on delivery. You haven't signed the contract yet. Nothing is secure without a contract." I couldn't help it; I admit that I'm idealistic. I believed everything this radio producer told me. Why would he lie to me, I thought. Months later, it all fell apart. Actually, it kind of blew up in my face.

HARD LESSONS

The radio producer turned from nicest guy in the world into meanest guy in the world. He told me that the project wasn't going forward and that I was the reason. After months of compliments and praise, now he said my gift wasn't good enough, that I didn't have what it takes. He said his last show was in Canada with a medium who was much better than me. He hung up the phone, leaving me shocked, vulnerable and defeated.

Ouch! That hurt. And it seemed to come out of nowhere. Bret and Bob agreed that the project must have fallen through for the guy and he was now blaming me. We later learned that this was exactly the case. But before we knew this, I took the man's criticisms to heart. For the first time since I began doing *The Spirit Communication Hour* on my own, I doubted myself. Maybe I really *wasn't* any good. I completely disregarded that Bob had worked with the most gifted mediums in the world and placed me in the same category. But that's how my twisted mind works. Bob was a friend, I told myself, and he had to say those things. But anyone who knows Bob knows that he wouldn't do that. I reasoned that this radio producer was a stranger and would therefore be more honest. So I punished myself until we learned the real reason the show was canceled, which wasn't even related to me. I guess it made the producer feel better to blame things on me rather than take responsibility for things himself.

My next experience, with the documentary filmmaker, was more positive. He's a sweet man with immense passion for his work. He has a clear vision of the message he wants to convey and he has never strayed from it. It is the same vision he articulated so clearly in his first email to Bob (as seen in the prior chapter). The only problem with documentary filmmaking is all the funding needed to keep the project afloat. These aren't big budget productions. The filmmaker obtained small grants to film the project, but it wasn't enough. As a result, the documentary has been on and off as funding for it trickles in. At one point, he announced that the project was being shut down completely until some undetermined date. I think he was simply frustrated and overwhelmed, because only a few months later, it was back in full swing again.

The film producer who filmed my four-show TV series on the UPN/WB network was from Maine. He was nice man, but not a Hollywood mover and shaker with lots of experience and connections to get things done. He was perfect for the first series, but over his head when it came to a national show—and he was the first to admit it. Although we talked with the local network that ran my first series, they unexpectedly found themselves in a poor position to move forward with an ongoing contract. They were having issues at the time that had them losing their local news program as a result. It was not a good time to negotiate a new show on spirit communication when they couldn't even keep their news program.

The producer did have an old friend who was a producer in Hollywood. He hadn't been in touch with him for twenty years, but he felt it couldn't hurt to call and see if he might be interested in representing my show. He made the call and the Hollywood producer was immediately interested. After viewing the tapes of my four-show series, he sent a contract. I signed the dotted line and waited… and waited and waited. Nothing happened. After about six months, I realized that I signed a contract with a producer whom I knew very little about. I didn't know his reputation. I didn't know his success rate. I didn't even know if he had the connections necessary to do what he promised. I took the local producer's word that this guy was legit, but what did he know? He was as ignorant about Hollywood as me, and he hadn't seen this guy for twenty years. I suddenly realized we were just two clueless New Englanders who were feeling their way through the dark corridors of Hollywood.

Around the sixth month, I had heard a lot of talk from the Hollywood producer but saw no results, not even one meeting with a network executive. Out of the blue, he proposed that he be my manager. I became confused: was he a producer or a manager? He admitted not having any experience as a manager, yet he wanted fifteen percent of all my income, expected me to pay all his expenses and told me not to expect any significant results for the first two years. I began to realize that I might have been wasting my time with this guy. In fact, it occurred to me that I had wasted a lot of time and energy with several people who were just like him. Yet I had no one to blame but myself because the deals that went sour all had one thing in common—my intuition had tried telling me to be cautious. Yet, every time, I jumped in head first with a big smile of denial on my face.

INCREASED WISDOM

In an earlier chapter, I described how I came into my personal power by facing my fears and challenging myself in spite of them. The experiences I just mentioned certainly tested those feelings of empowerment; but even more, they reminded me to trust my instincts. My desire to accomplish my goals all at once, without going through the necessary steps, drowned out that inner voice that was giving me a yellow light to slow down and proceed with caution. I wanted to teach the world that we need not fear death, that it is just a transition and not an end. But I wanted to do it overnight. So when a few people came along promising to help me accomplish that goal, I ignored my intuition and placed my power into their hands.

In effect, I had put the progress I was making on hold until I learned the lesson and took my power back.

In many ways, I have been very lucky. Nobody has really taken advantage of me to a devastating consequence. The only thing I have lost is time and money. And, like with any loss, I have gained wisdom from the lessons learned.

Part of the wisdom I gained is that life is like a book, and we have to go page by page, chapter by chapter, in order to gain its full benefit. I wanted to skip chapters and get right to the end. I couldn't wait to see how it all unfolded. I accuse myself of being too anxious. I was so focused on reaching the largest audience possible with my message that I wanted to skip steps, skip from Chapter Six to the Conclusion. However, it wasn't money or fame that interested me; it was personal fulfillment. I get so much fulfillment from touching souls with my work that I wanted to touch the maximum number possible in the least amount of time. Yet this desire—this craving—had a price. It didn't hurt others, but it could have hurt me. By skipping ahead, I would have missed out on the knowledge and compassion that comes from experiencing each person and every experience that life has to offer in a journey—one word, one page, one chapter at a time.

CHAPTER NINETEEN
LITERARY AGENTS, THE SLUSH PILE &
COMING FULL CIRCLE

By Bob Olson

When spider webs unite, they can tie up a lion.

~ Ethiopian Proverb

A year-and-a-half after starting OfSpirit.com, which was about three years after first meeting Vicki, I felt I had enough content to complete my book. While the first half of the book was about my transforming experiences with Vicki, the second half described other mediums I had met and the unique and interesting ways they each used their gift. One medium was a "spirit artist" who could draw portraits of the spirits with whom she linked. Another offered messages directly from her own spirit guides, messages that offered a deeper insight into the purpose of your life and relationships. And, still, another presented an educational stage demonstration with the precision and entertainment of a Broadway play, except with spirits as his costars.

By the time I finished the manuscript titled, *Medium Rare: A Skeptic's Journey Into The World Of Psychic Mediums And The Afterlife*, I had twenty chapters and three appendixes. It documented almost all my experiences with psychic mediums over the course of three years. Using stories to teach what I had learned about spirit communication and spirit messengers, it revealed a wide-range of discoveries. Many mediums who read it told me that they learned things about mediums and mediumship that even they never knew. Now it was time to find a literary agent.

LITERARY AGENT #1: IT WAS MEANT TO BE

I had targeted a literary agent to represent me. I had been following his career for six years and knew he was the agent for me. Right before sending him my proposal, I noticed that his wife—who handled all the spiritual books for his literary agency—had the same birthday as Vicki. The coincidence was unbelievable. In fact, her birthday was in four days. I express-mailed my book proposal in an envelope marked, "Happy Birthday." Of course, I explained the coincidence in my cover letter so as to not appear entirely scheming. Then, just two days after FedEx-ing my book proposal to them, the agent emailed me asking me to send my manuscript as soon as possible. Yes! I was in the flow. I was being guided.

I express-mailed the manuscript marked with bright permanent marker "Requested Material" just as he instructed. Then I waited. After a month, I sent an email asking if they got the manuscript. I got a reply. It read, "Yes." That was it, "Yes." Not a "We love it!" or "We are still reading it;" or even "We are presently laughing at your manuscript. It sucks!" Just "Yes."

I waited another month. Then I emailed again, but this time I got no reply. "Oh no, I'm being too pushy," I thought. I had read that literary agents are very busy and don't like pushy authors. I decided to sit tight. After all, they had requested my manuscript in just two days after receiving my proposal. Plus, there was the whole birthday coincidence thing; it was meant to be... so I wanted to believe.

THE SLUSH PILE? I'M NOT SUPPOSED TO BE IN THE SLUSH PILE!

I originally sent my manuscript to the agent in early October. By late January—yes, I had been extremely patient—I got a call on the phone. It was her, the agent's wife who handled all the spiritual books. However, she wasn't calling about my manuscript; she was calling to see if I would be interested in ghostwriting books for her. I was confused. I asked her to clarify. She told me that she was starting a new division in the agency to package books. She was looking for spiritual authors. So she asked her assistant to go into the "slush pile" to find some well-written authors she could contact.

Slush pile? I wasn't supposed to be in the slush pile. The slush pile is for unsolicited manuscripts—manuscripts that people just mail to agents without sending a proposal first. My book wasn't supposed to be in the slush pile; they asked me to send it, damn it!

I didn't know whether to be happy or angry. I contained myself and proceeded to ask about my manuscript. She didn't know anything about it. She certainly hadn't read it. But after a half-hour conversation, she promised she would. And then she kept promising by email every couple weeks. By the end of February, I realized it was all a cosmic joke. I figured God, my spirit guides or my father—maybe everybody up there—was having a good laugh at my expense. I took it as a lesson. I'm still not sure what the lesson is, but I took it as a lesson.

LITERARY AGENT #2: AGAINST MY INTUITION

I quickly found another literary agent, which turned out to be another joke. This agent was embarrassed by the subject matter. Oh, he didn't actually come out and say that, but he did admit to me that he was still a skeptic. It became obvious that he was embarrassed about the subject matter when he talked about his conversations with editors at publishing companies. He didn't want these editors whom he had to face all the time thinking he was a "believer."

Of course, my intuition had screamed to me that this was not a good match in my first conversation with this agent. But I was frustrated and didn't want to listen to what my gut was telling me. Long story short, after nine months with him, I decided that *Medium Rare* wasn't going to happen. Heck, by this time, almost four years after I first met Vicki, I realized that mediums were not really all that "rare" anyway. After all, I knew oodles of them.

I finally made the decision to terminate my contract with this agent. I expect he was probably relieved. In hindsight, I realized that I had tried giving him a pep talk every time we spoke on the phone. I don't think an author is supposed to have to do that. If the agent isn't enthusiastic about a book, he shouldn't be representing it. It was a valuable lesson I needed to learn.

WHAT ARE WE WAITING FOR?

Then one day, Melissa and I went out to dinner with Vick and Bret. Vicki had a lot of exciting things happening in her life but she was frustrated. She was tired of waiting for people. She had done a four-show series on television and now had a producer pitching an ongoing series to the major networks, but almost a year had gone by with no results. She also had a documentary filmmaker who had started a documentary about her life more than eighteen months prior. The filmmaker had obtained some grants but still struggled with funding. As a result, the documentary was on-again off-again. Like my experience with the literary agents, Vicki was fed up waiting for people.

We laughed about our frustrations with Hollywood and the publishing industry, and commented on the humility of it all. Someone came up with the idea that we should do a book together. Vicki had an agent who was going to handle a book for her, but that meant more waiting. We began to realize we didn't need to depend on others anymore.

We asked ourselves why either of us was waiting for other people to make things happen. I had created one of the largest Internet resources in the holistic, spiritual and self-improvement field. Vicki had a long-running radio show that topped the ratings. I had created and promoted major events selling hundreds of tickets. Vicki had presented and promoted sell-out medium demonstrations to hundreds of people. I had even sold my first book to a publisher without an agent. And Vicki sold her four-part television series to a network without an agent. We realized we could do this book on our own. Heck, we could start our own publishing company if we had to!

So we decided to write a book together. I would use a few chapters from *Medium Rare* and write some new ones. Vicki would determine what she wanted to convey and I'd help her with the writing. It felt right, and we started on it the very next Monday. We were nearing the four-year anniversary of my first reading with Vicki. How appropriate that we should begin doing radio interviews and events together again to promote a book.

It took us four years, but we had now come full circle. And we had learned so much in the interim. Vicki had a spiritual knowing but needed to find the power of her human spirit. She did it. I had found the power of my human spirit but needed a spiritual knowing. I did it. In the end, we both got what we needed. Two very separate journeys, yet leading to the same result—each understanding our Self. This is what makes life exciting! We started together, moved in separate directions and now met again to begin a *new* journey.

CHAPTER TWENTY
UNDERSTANDING SPIRIT,
UNDERSTANDING YOURSELF

By Bob Olson & Vicki Monroe

The grand difficulty is to feel the reality of both worlds, so as to give each its due place in our thoughts and feelings: to keep our mind's eye and our heart's eye ever fixed on the land of promise, without looking away from the road along which we are to travel toward it.

~ August W. and Julius C. Hare

The stories Vicki and I have shared with you in this book do not fit tightly into one neat and narrow message. That is because these stories are real, not fictional. It is also because there are *many* important messages we hope you have gained from this book. Nevertheless, we have tried to extract two key messages that we have learned from our journeys, which we would like to emphasize to you in this final chapter.

KEY MESSAGE #1: WE DO NOT DIE

First, Vicki and I believe that one of the most important lessons we have gained in our experiences is that life is eternal—we do not die. This means that we are not our bodies, that our bodies are merely vehicles to carry us through life. And when they eventually slow down, break down and stop working, we will not cease to exist; but rather, we will move beyond our physical existence here on the earth plane and return to our natural state, which is spirit.

This means that heaven is home to us. The spirit world is where we originated and where we truly belong. So death means "going home." Our earthly existence is only meant to be temporary in order to give us opportunities to learn and grow. For some reason, our spiritual growth is faster here on earth. And while it is almost a cliché to say that life is like going away to college, that comparison is one of the best analogies we have.

When you understand that we don't die—that life is a temporary place of learning—then you also begin to understand that our deceased loved ones still exist. And as you move forward in your discoveries about the afterlife, you learn that our loved ones in spirit are always with us. They know what we are doing, saying and even feeling. Therefore, we are not separated from them when they pass on; we simply must learn new ways of communicating with them.

Talking to our loved ones in spirit is easy. They hear everything we think and say. Hearing them is our challenge. And while there are a variety of methods for receiving messages from spirit—including prayer, meditation, automatic writing and dreams—mediumship is one means of communication that can be extremely valuable for those who still need more evidence before they are ready to start listening on their own.

On the other side of this spiritual knowing that *we don't die* comes an inner feeling of peace with our *own* death. When we discover that this life is not the be-all and end-all of existence, it is comforting to know that we will still exist when we die, that our deceased loved ones will greet us when we cross over, and that our "true home" is filled with joy, love and ecstasy that is beyond our human ability to comprehend.

KEY MESSAGE #2: WE MUST BALANCE OUR SPIRITUAL SELF WITH OUR HUMAN SELF

Do you remember in your youth when you were with a good friend but were totally focused on some guy or girl with whom you had a crush? If you thought about it later, you probably realized that you totally missed the pleasure of being with your friend because you were not fully present. Instead, you were focused on someone else.

You have probably experienced other moments when you were so focused on the past or the future that you totally missed the joy of the present moment. Perhaps you were at the park with your children or out to dinner with your spouse, but your mind was still at work, worrying about the bills or focused on what somebody said or did to you.

In the same way, it is very common that when people begin to learn about matters of spirit, they focus most of their time, thoughts and energy on their spiritual self, thereby ignoring their human self. While it is important to understand matters of spirit, it is also important to understand matters of human spirit. And so our second key message to you is to not lose sight of your human self by focusing too much on your spiritual self.

We are living a human existence. As stated in the Introduction, the underlying message of this book is that life is about balancing matters of spirit with matters of human spirit. We can't live in this world focused on just one or the other. We are originally from spirit, yet we are living inside human bodies among a society of human beings. Even the adage that says, "We are not human beings having a spiritual experience, but rather spiritual beings having a human experience," does not mean we must only focus on the spiritual. It means we must remember the importance of both.

THE NEED FOR UNDERSTANDING OUR SPIRITUAL SELF: BOB'S STORY

By the time I was in my late twenties, I had found the power of my human spirit. I was ambitious, successful and physically fit. Yet I lacked a spiritual knowing. Then at the age of twenty-seven, I was given an opportunity to recognize this imbalance. I fell into a chronic depression due to a brain disorder—a biological chemical imbalance in my brain.

For five years, my depression deepened as doctors struggled to find a treatment that would work for me. After the first year, I was so depressed that I could no longer work. I remained disabled from working for the next four years. I became socially phobic and began to sleep an average of eighteen hours a day. By the fourth year, I was suicidal and losing hope that I would ever escape the confines of my mental hell. I had tried over fifteen medications, and combinations of those medications, and endured twenty-one electroshock treatments during my five-year struggle without success. Some doctors began to label me "treatment resistant."

In the fifth year, I finally found a medication to beat my brain disorder and lift my debilitating depression. Two months later I was back to work, partying with my friends and feeling more energy and joy than I had ever felt in my life. I have now been symptom-free since 1994, over nine blessed years as I write this.

Since my story was an inspiring account of the power of the human spirit, I wrote a book about it that was published in 1999. But while writing that book, I recognized a need for spiritual insight to help me make sense of my suffering. I also recognized that a deeper spiritual connection would have helped me during my ordeal, as well.

My experience with depression taught me that while the power of my human spirit gave me the strength to cope with my disorder and to have the persistence to find a treatment to end my suffering, it also taught me of my need for spiritual insight and a spiritual connection that would have provided me with increased hope, comfort and understanding during my dark night of the soul.

THE NEED FOR UNDERSTANDING OUR HUMAN SELF: VICKI'S STORY

Vicki, too, had an experience that opened her eyes to the imbalance she had about her human spirit. By the time Vicki was in his early thirties, she had a deep spiritual knowing, yet she lacked a connection to her personal power. Then she was given an opportunity to recognize this imbalance when she discovered a passion and purpose within her gift of spirit communication.

By the time Vicki discovered her true calling—her purpose as a spirit messenger—she found herself unprepared and lacking in how to express it. When she finally realized that the gift she had known since she was a child had taught her insights about spirits and the spirit world that other people craved, she was overcome with a desire to spread her message. Yet she had no idea how to do it. She was looking over a sea of souls who needed what she had to offer, but she was without a clue on how to reach them or teach them.

Imagine the frustration of finally realizing your soul's mission—of knowing that you have an ability and insight that can relieve people's suffering and fear by offering hope, understanding and a spiritual connection—yet you feel powerless to spread your message without the help of another.

And then you realize that you have no idea who to ask for help anyway.

This, of course, is where Vicki and I were in our individual quests for balance when we met. My first book was published within days of my initial reading with Vicki. Vicki's third professional reading appointment was with me. There is no coincidence that Vicki and I met at this moment in our lives when we recognized a need for balance, and then, suddenly, we met the person who could teach us what we needed in order to obtain that balance.

Vicki and I connected to teach one another the lessons we each needed to learn. If we only needed the power of spirit, Vicki's story would be different. If we only needed the power of human spirit, my story would be different. Instead, we each needed to discover that aspect of our self that was missing in order to find the ultimate power that comes from internalizing a balance between the two.

CONCLUSION: A FUNNY THING HAPPENED ON OUR WAY TO BALANCE

As Vicki and I found balance, something occurred that almost went unnoticed. By balancing these areas where we were lacking, we also enhanced those parts of ourselves with which we each began.

When Vicki finally discovered her personal power, her readings, radio shows and stage demonstrations improved to a level she never knew was possible. When I finally gained my spiritual "knowing," my work as a writer, speaker and magazine editor also improved to a level of which I never knew was possible. Somehow the natural gifts that we honed early in life were now exponentially potent as a result of finding balance in that area of understanding *spirit* or understanding *human spirit* where we lacked.

So whether your own personal journey is to discover the power of your human self or to discover the power of your spiritual self, you can also expect your life to transform in every area of your being as you continue to learn and grow. That is why we titled this book *Understanding Spirit, Understanding Yourself.*

With love, hope and peace,
Bob Olson & Vicki Monroe

I am not going to die. I'm going home like a shooting star.

~ *Sojourner Truth*

RECOMMENDED READING

The Complete Idiot's Guide(R) to Communicating with Spirits
By Rita Berkowitz
Paperback: 360 pages; Alpha Books; 1st edition (August 27, 2002)
ISBN: 002864350X

How to Get a Good Reading from a Psychic Medium
By Carole Lynne
Paperback: 121 pages; Red Wheel/Weiser; (April 2003)
ISBN: 1578632919

Born Knowing: A Medium's Journey-Accepting and Embracing My Spiritual Gifts
By John Holland
Paperback: ; Hay House; (March 2003)
ISBN: 1401900828

Hello from Heaven!
By Bill Guggenheim, Judy Guggenheim
Mass Market Paperback: 416 pages; Bantam Books (May 1999)
ISBN: 0553576348

We Don't Die: George Anderson's Conversations With the Other Side
By Joel Martin and Patricia Romanowski

Mass Market Paperback: 289 pages; Berkley Pub Group (March 1989)
ISBN: 0425114511

A World Beyond: A Startling Message from the Eminent Psychic Arthur Ford from Beyond the Grave
By Ruth Montgomery
Mass Market Paperback: 176 pages; Fawcett Books (October 1989)
ISBN: 044920832X

Many Lives, Many Masters
by Brian Weiss
Paperback: 224 pages; Fireside (July 1988)
ISBN: 0671657860

Talking to Heaven: A Medium's Message of Life After Death
By James Van Praagh
Mass Market Paperback: 292 pages; Penguin USA (March 1999)
ISBN: 0451191722

Life After Life : The Investigation of a Phenomenon—Survival of Bodily Death
by Raymond Moody
Paperback: 208 pages; Harper SanFrancisco (March 6, 2001)
ISBN: 0062517392

Journey of Souls: Case Studies of Life Between Lives
by Michael Duff Newton
Paperback: 278 pages; Llewellyn Publications; (July 1994)
ISBN: 1567184855

The Other Side and Back: A Psychic's Guide to Our World and Beyond
by Sylvia Browne
Mass Market Paperback: 274 pages; Signet (July 10, 2000)
ISBN: 0451198638

One Last Time: A Psychic Medium Speaks to Those We Have Loved and Lost
by John Edward
Paperback: 231 pages; Berkley Pub Group; (February 2000)
ISBN: 0425166929

Lessons from the Light: Extraordinary Messages of Comfort and Hope from the Other Side
by George Anderson, Andrew Barone
Paperback: 321 pages; Berkley Pub Group (February 2000)
ISBN: 0425174166

Walking in the Garden of Souls: George Anderson's Advice from the Hereafter, for Living in the Here and Now
by George Anderson, Andrew Barone
Paperback: 272 pages; Berkley Pub Group (October 2002)
ISBN: 0425186113

Saved by the Light
by Dannion Brinkley
Mass Market Paperback: 224 pages; Harper Mass Market Paperbacks (March 1995)
ISBN: 0061008893

Win The Battle, The 3-Step Lifesaving Formula to Conquer Depression and Bipolar Disorder
by Bob Olson, Melissa Olson
Hardcover: 156 pages; Chandler House Press; (January 1999)
ISBN: 1886284318

CONTACT INFORMATION

Vicki Monroe
(207) 499-0067
vicki@vickimonroe.com
www.VickiMonroe.com

Bob Olson
(207) 967-9892
editor@ofspirit.com
www.OfSpirit.com
www.GriefAndBelief.com
www.BestPsychicMediums.com